Politics of Ethnicity and Governance in South Sudan

Understanding the complexity of the World's newest Country

John Adoor Deng

The Politics of Ethnicity and Governance in South: Understanding the Complexity of the World's newest Country

Copyright © John Adoor Deng, 2016

First published 2016.
This edition published by Africa World Books, 2017.

All rights reserved. Without limiting the rights under copyright reserved above, no part of this publication may be reproduced, stored in or introduced into a database and retrieval system or transmitted in any form or any means (electronic, mechanical, photocopying, recording or otherwise) without the prior written permission of both the owner of copyright and the above publishers.

National Library of Australia Cataloguing-in-Publication entry

Creator: Deng, John Adoor, author.

Title: The politics of ethnicity and governance in South Sudan: understanding the complexity of the world's newest country / John Adoor Deng.

ISBN: 978-0-9876141-7-9

Subjects: Political development. Ethnicity--Political aspects--South Sudan. South Sudan--Politics and government.

Dewey Number: 320.9629

Published with the assistance of:

www.loveofbooks.com.au

Contents

About the Author v
Dedication vii
Abbreviations viii
Figures ix
Foreword x
Acknowledgements xii
Abstract xiv
Introduction.................................1
Brief background of ethnic grouping 3
Ethnic group's role during wars of liberation 17
   The emergence of first civil war in Sudan..........20
   Addis Ababa Agreement 23
   The emergence of second civil war...............25
   Rebellions within Rebellion 26
   Comprehensive Peace Agreement, 2005...........29
Negative ethnic politics.......................32
   Theories underpinning tribalism and conflicts 37
   Political ethnically motivated conflict..............44
Religious contribution to ethnic conflicts 53
   The role of religion in civil unrest and wars........60
South Sudan as failed and fragile State 70

Institutional Reforms and Good Governance 80
Good Governance 82
Institutional reforms as a recipe for reconstituting good governance 93
   1. Applying the rule of law 93
   2. Reducing land grabbing vice................94
   3. Instituting proper taxation system............96
   4. SPLM should not be a political party 97
   5. SPLA should be made a conventional national army 101
   6. Establishment of Multicultural Commission. . .103
   7. Establishing National Integrated Educational Curriculum 104
   8. Empowering traditional leadership structure ..105
   9. Install federalism in the right time 106
References **112**

About the Author

John Adoor Deng was born in Jonglei State, South Sudan in a Payam call Wanglei in Twic East County. He is a member of an extended family of 42 siblings, (brothers and sisters), an origin of African traditional polygamous family of 7 wives. His father Deng Ngon Deng was naturally born humanitarian person, well-known for courage, bravery and for sharing his wealth with all persons especially the needy in the greater Bor and beyond. John is believed to have inherited blessings of good luck from his father although he did not win the lotto! John catches opportunities quickly, in a very short time, he has achieved many goals in his lifetime as a young man; a father of 6 beautiful children (two boys and four girls) with his beloved wife, Sarah Achol Malual.

In Australia, John has contributed enormously to the settlement of migrants and Refugee Communities. He founded and directs Sudanese Support Foundation (SSF), an organization that provides support services to people in needs; offer support in literacy, housing, employment and promoting integrative social services. In this works, he had received numerous awards for outstanding works from local, state and federal governments in Australia. Also, Mr. Deng has worked in various levels of governments in Australia, as community development officer at the Brisbane City Council. Customer

Service Advisor (CSA) at the Federal Department of Human Service. In recent years, he was also employed as Community Education Liaison Officer at the Queensland State Department of Education, Training, and the Arts. On the weekends, John volunteers as a minister in the Anglican Parish of Goodna where he since 2007 operate as an Anglican Associate Minister and a head of Sudanese Australian Anglican Ministry (SAAM).

At the community level, John was a founding member of Queensland African Communities Council (QACC); he was once a president of Sudanese Community Association of Queensland Inc. (SUCAQ) and elected interim chairman of the Federation of South Sudanese Australian Communities (FOSSCA). In the academics, John has studied Cert 4 Training and Assessment at TAFE, Diploma of Theological Studies, Bible College of East Africa, Bachelor of Theological Studies, Vision International University (VIU), Bachelor of Social Science, (QUT), Master of Public Relations, University of Southern Queensland (USQ), Master of Politics and Public Policy at Macquarie University, and Master of Management at the University of Southern Queensland (USQ). He is a proud South Sudanese Australian and he appreciates the privilege of holding two citizenships (Australia & South Sudan) dearly. John hopes to be a scholar and academician with the aim to work with universities and especially to build the capacity of national universities in the Republic of South Sudan.

Dedication

This book is dedicated to the younger generation of South Sudanese upon which the future of the country belongs. History has shown that generations come, and generations go, and they both left their footprints, legacies, whether positive or negative to the proceeding posterity. I, therefore, with this understanding dedicate this noble book to my daughter Margaret Aguil Adoor's generation and the generation after.

It is my sincere wish that this little book contributes to the debates around the de-ethnicization of South Sudan politics in this century and hopefully for those times to come. I am hoping that the readers of this book shall find common perspectives and a challenge to their grown up ways of thinking, perspectives, and world views in relations to ethnicity.

Abbreviations

SPLM – Sudan People Liberation Movement
SPLA – Sudan People Liberation Army
USQ – University of Southern Queensland
CPA – Comprehensive Peace Agreement
NCP – National Congress Party
SSLM – Southern Sudan Liberation Movement
WCC – World Council of Churches
AACC – All African Conference of Churches
YATIA – Youth against Tribalism in Africa
SSTV – South Sudan Tele-Vision
SLM/A – Sudan Liberation Movement
SLA – Sudan Liberation Army
JEM – Justice and Equality Movement
ATR – African Traditional Religion
SSCC – South Sudan Council of Churches
OCHA – Office for the Coordination of Humanitarian Affairs
PB – Political Bureau
NLC – National Liberation Council
SPLM-DC – Sudan People Liberation Movement for Democratic Change
SPLM-FD – Sudan People Liberation Movement Former Detainees

SPLM-IO – Sudan People Liberation Movement in Opposition
LC – Letters of Credit
COH – Cessation of Hostilities

Figures

Figure 1: Tribal groups in South Sudan – 6

Figure 2: Cattle raiding matrix – 33

Figure3: Dinka and Nuer Contemporary political conflicts – 39

Figure 4: Main Religious Groups in South Sudan – 45

Figure 5: Factors contributing to internal religious conflicts – 48

Figure 6: Contemporary religious inclined conflicts – 51

Figure 7: Twelve social and economic indicators – 60

Figure 8: Lewin's planned change models – 67

Figure 9: Characteristics of good governance – 76

Foreword

From the political landscape of South Sudan came a man of great integrity and passion for community. In his first book, Rev John Adoor Deng explains the complex nature of how local ethnic groups of South Sudan are influencing and shaping a nation of people who have lived through a civil war and who then democratically elected the Government of South Sudan following independence.

John uses his personal knowledge as Civil War survivor to effectually portray and explain politics in South Sudan. I first met John around 2008 when he was establishing the Sudanese Support Foundation, over the years I have talked with him about being a migrant to Australia.

When South Sudan was voting on independence we had some discussions on the benefits, however, this book delves into the depths and intricacies of human nature, the politics that underpin the policies, structures, and machinery of government that is working to shape a modern South Sudan. John has worked tirelessly in Australia, particularly for people from the South Sudan to enable them to settle into a life in Australia.

In 2013, John was the recipient of a City of Ipswich Medallion at the Ipswich City Council's Australia Day awards. The award recognized Mr. Deng's work in setting up the Sudanese Support Foundation which helps to raise money for prosthetic limbs for Sudanese victims maimed by the civil war, as well as assisting with settlement services, community engagement and development for people from South Sudan who have chosen to make Ipswich their home.

Cr Kerry Silver

Councillor for Division 3

Ipswich City Council

Acknowledgements

When thinking about what to do to contribute to the debates on ethnic politics and conflicts in South Sudan, the idea of writing this book came into my mind. Although as a periodic commentator on political, social, religious and economic issues in the Republic of South Sudan, I felt it was still good addition to writing this little book that I have entirely dedicated to the Younger People of South Sudan. The writing of this book was therefore precipitated by constant news of tribal conflicts in the country that without exaggeration, appear on the weekly and monthly basis in both social and public media. These conflicts have continued to take innocent lives and maimed citizens of our country. I am aware that considerable volumes of books have been written within the context of ethnic debates in Africa as a whole and South Sudan, in particular.

Hence, this book shall serve as an addition to this critical area of debate on the continent and the Republic of South Sudan primarily. It is my wish that this little book contributes to the debates around the de-ethnicization of South Sudan politics in this century and hopefully for the proceeding centuries. I anticipate and hope that the readers of this book shall find a common inspiring perspective and a challenge to their grown-up ways of thinking geared towards ethnic groups.

An Australian artist once stated in his lyrics that "from little things, big things grow," the artist seems to suggest that small initiatives indeed in some cases, have the potential to produce great progress. Similarly, I believe that from this little script, something inspirational may grow, as a result. I fully acknowledge the role that my dear beloved family has played during the writing of this book.

Truthfully, I would not have done anything had my family not been on my side. I thank my beautiful wife Sarah Achol Malual, for having given me time and opportunities to concentrate on working on my book while she took the oversize role in taking care of our family. I thank my young son David Deng Adoor for checking on me each time especially with this question "Dad are you OK?" I am indebted to say a big thank you to my daughter Monica Yar Adoor who at the point of my tiredness, tabled coffee to energize and stimulate my reflective thinking. On a professional level, I thank my colleagues from the University of Southern Queensland (USQ), especially Mr. Oroto Lamero and Mr. Chol Aleu. The intellectual discussions we have had, did in effect endow my initial inspiration to write this book. Indeed, this development would not have proceeded triumphantly without the backing of supporters and enablers in the professional world.

On this note, I thank the printing press, editors, workmates and donors who have contributed the finalization of this book. Indeed, these bits, here and there, have undoubtedly contributed to the energies that have made me stronger and full of confidence to finish up this text. I, therefore, say a big thank you to you all; even those that my memory cannot bring to light and have in some way or another contributed. Note that your support is valued and highly appreciated. Your help remained in my psyche in this life.

Notes: *Australian Artist "From little things, big things grow"*

Abstract

This little book documents the brief history of contemporary South Sudanese politics within the context of the 22 years of the second war of liberation. A portion of it explores 17 years of the first Sudanese civil war that ended in 1972 through the Addis-Abba Agreement. The book has made the meaningful analysis of the governance after the birth of the World's newest Republic (South Sudan). It is divided into seven major chapters. Each chapter addresses the unique context of the South Sudanese political, civil, religious and military life. Chapter one introduces the book in its etymological context to the reader and chapter two narrates on ethnic groupings in South Sudan. Chapter three explores the significant roles played by ethnic groups during the war of liberation in South Sudan and beyond. This chapter appreciates positive contributions made by various ethnic groups in supporting the war efforts.

In chapter four, the author teased the negative politics rendered in ethnic context and explained how that negativity resulted in bloodshed of innocent civilians. In this chapter, some theories that have aided negative ethnic politics in the country have been discussed. Chapter five addresses religious significance and explores its negative role in fueling conflicts and feuds in South Sudan and elsewhere in the world. A significant part of this chapter is dedicated to the discussion of South Sudan as a failed state in chapter six; and as a country born in the 21st century, many analysts have argued that South Sudan has double-jumped to top the world's failed and fragile states. The book concludes with suggestions for institutional reforms in a quest to install good governance in the Republic of South Sudan.

Chapter One
Introduction

South Sudan is a country made up of 64 tribes groups, scattered across the recently instituted ten states of South Sudan. The country is, therefore, one of the most ethnic, multicultural and diverse countries in the world. This social fabric continues to be regarded as the essential nature-given gift for all citizens in the country. However, in recent years, the world's newest state has adopted a blended culture of ethnic hatred and negative politics of ethnicization. Hence, it is the sole purpose of this book to attempting to de-ethnicitize the politics of South Sudan in this century.

I am a believer in social harmony and respectful relations between tribes and communities. I argue against negative ethnicization of politics in Africa and South Sudan, in particular. The facts reinforce this belief that ethnically-based conflicts in effect plug the nations into the unprepared breaking of conventional bonds; disintegrate it into despicable and loathsome situations. The world is watching South Sudan in disbelief as the country has embarked on tribally engineered conflicts, losing the direction of ethnic harmony, engaging in ethnic hatred, ethnic cleansing, and killing of each other on the pretext of tribal origin. Thus, this book recommends possible prospects for building stronger political will around the notion of de-ethnicization of politics in the Republic of South Sudan.

In current human civilization, it is clear that nations are made up primarily of families, individuals and clans, which translate into groups, tribes, associations, societies, communities and, therefore, a government. These categories remain critically important as they serve as what I refer to as standing pillars that hold the nation in firm stability. For that substantial balance to remain intact, these posts ought to exist in the web of interconnectedness so that cohesiveness becomes the mode in a circle. The additional purposes of this book are to explore how some of these very pillars are turned into dismantling tools resulting in the loss of lives of innocent masses under merciless militias on both sides of the conflict.

This book shall explore the brief background of ethnic groups in South Sudan; shed light on the roles played by ethnic groups in all wars of liberation in Sudan and then Southern Sudan; detail the triggers of negative ethnic politics in South Sudan, discuss the weight of the contribution made by religious categories; expose how ethnicity should be regarded as a positive thing; and finally recommend institutional contribution into ethnic harmonization in the country.

References

http://www.southsudannation.com/proposed-. (2014). Proposed federal system for future South Sudan.

http://www.independentnetwork.org.uk/press/largest-number-independents-120-years. (2014). Largest number of independents in 120 years standing.

Chapter Two
Brief background of ethnic grouping

Before gaining her independence in 2011, South Sudan was an integral part of the modern Republic of Sudan. The South region was predominantly inhabited by culturally and linguistically diverse black African tribes, making South Sudan an ancestral home to about 64 major ethnic groups. It is estimated that about 40% of the South population speaks Dinka dialect also known as thuong-Jang. Dinka is one of the Nilo-Saharan languages spoken in South Sudan. The other 60% of the South Sudan population speak other languages including Nuer, Luo, and the Ubangian family which occupies the southwest of the country. For example, the Ubangian language spoken in South Sudan is in Western Equatoria. It is also believed that there are 80 sub-ethnic groups in South Sudan. These sub-ethnic groups are distinguished by dialects and languages.

In one tribe, you can find more small groups speaking different dialects typically based on the geographical area. As for leadership and governance issues; in some tribes, the elders are more judicial in nature, with Chiefs dealing with conflict resolution. Some tribes are locally concentrated in one region in South Sudan, and others are part of groups that spread across several national boundaries. To maintain ethnic harmony in a part of the world in which tribal conflict is relatively commonplace, one group has proposed the creation of a

"House of Nationalities" to represent all 64 recognized groups in Juba (Demographic of South Sudan).

President Salva Kiir Mayardit declared at the ceremony marking South Sudanese independence on 9 July 2011 that the country "should have a new beginning of tolerance where cultural and ethnic diversity will be a source of pride (Kiir, 2011)." This diversity is a present reality in most African countries. Ethnic groups serve as primary social units in the country. The Nilotic people occupy a vast land in South Sudan and are considered to be majority group in the country. They include tribes such as Dinka, Nuer, Toposa, and the Shilluk. Other Nilotic people with similar cultures and traditions live in neighbouring countries especially in the south-western part of Ethiopia, the north-eastern part of Uganda, the western part of Kenya, and the northern part Tanzania respectively.

Historically, the Nilotic family value cattle as a primary economic resource used for many essential transactions including dowry payment in marriages. Cattle are rare commodities in these communities; it sometimes led to cattle raiding and stealing for one to have cattle. With this civilization, some of these cultures may fade away speed; few cases in recent years have seen marriages entirely facilitated with money.

In South Sudan, the Non-Nilotic group includes the Azande, Murle, Didinga, Tennet, Moru, Madi, and Balanda respectively. Although, these tribes share similar cultures and traditions, nonetheless each tribe group has its unique sub-cultures, traditions, customs and system of governance culminating in each cluster having distinctive world views and contexts. For example, before the colonial era and subsequently the Arab domination, South Sudanese ethnic groups did not have a common language, let alone a unified system of governance that was regarded as a collective identity.

Each tribe group had its unwritten rules, customs and system of governance. It could not be undermining that under these disparities, there was concerted present of peace and harmony between neighbouring tribes groups. A good example is the fact the Nuer and Dinka tribes, especially in the greater Upper Nile, have existed for generations in a congenial relationship. However, history has recorded few brawls around cattle raiding, and competition over pastures (Toch), and issues relating to the mismanaged marriages. Marriages in the South Sudan cultures are highly esteemed both for the purpose of gaining wealth and as well as for procreation. It is expected that marriages are done in absolute conformity to traditional unwritten rules and regulations.

Thus any marriage that falls short of community expectations, precipitate conflict, and disputes. Neither eloping girls nor early pregnancy is tolerated in most South Sudanese communities. In those days, skirmishes caused by these practices were well sorted, and culprits disciplined unbiasedly.

In the Customary Laws of South Sudan, a narrative of tribes is well presented.

Dinka

The Dinka, one of the branches of the River Lake Nilotes, are a group of closely related peoples living in southern Sudan, concentrated in the Upper Nile province in south-east Sudan and across into south-west Ethiopia. They are the largest ethnic group in South Sudan and are made up of some smaller tribes, Dinka Malual, Twic, Rek, Ruweng, Bor, Agar, Atwot and Ngok Ablinug. The Dinka peoples speak a series of closely related languages, which are grouped by linguists into five broad families of dialects. The five languages are called Northeastern, Northwestern, Southeastern, Southwestern and

South Central. Each subgroup calls its speech by the group's name, and over thirty dialects have been identified among the five language groupings.

The Dinkas are agnatic, semi-nomadic cattle-herders. Cattle-herding in the open plains promotes a special way of life in which tensions between individuality and sociability, between aggression and social control, between generations, between father and son, become prominent. Polygamy is the ideal for the Dinka, though many men may have only one wife. The Dinka must marry outside their clan (exogamy), which promotes more cohesion across the broader Dinka group. "Bride wealth" is paid by the groom's family to finalise the marriage alliance between the two clan families. Levirate marriage provides support for widows and their children. All children of co-wives are raised together and have a wide family identity.

The Dinka believe in a single universal God, whom they call Nhialac. Humans contact Nhialic through spiritual intermediaries and entities called yath and jak, which can be manipulated by various rituals. They believe that the spirits of the departed become part of the spiritual sphere of this life. As well as being the fundamental measure of the wealth of Dinka society, cattle have religious significance. They are the first choice as an animal of sacrifice, though sheep may be sacrificed as a substitute on occasion. The family and general social relations are primary values in the Dinka religious thought. Unsurprisingly, much of Dinka customary law is inextricably linked to both cattle and the family.

Nuer

The Nuer, the second largest group of Nilotic people in South Sudan, live mainly in the east Upper Nile Province around the junction of the Nile River with the Bahr el Ghazal and Sobat Rivers and extending up the Sobat across the Ethiopian border. The [Nuer] people are related to the Dinka, who live to their west, and their culture is very similar. The Nuer, Dinka and Atwot (Atuot) are sometimes considered one ethnic group. The Nuer language is closely related to the speech of the Dinka and Atwot. The principal tribes of the Nuer are Jikany, Gawaar and Lou.

Like the Dinka, Nuer worldview is built around cattle and prestige is measured by the quantity and quality of the herd a man owns. Men and women take the names of their favourite bull or cow and prefer to be greeted by their cattle names. Parallel to territorial divisions are clan lineages descended through the male line from a single ancestor. These lineages are significant in the control and distribution of resources.

Marriages must be outside one's clan and are made legal by the payment of cattle by the man's clan to the woman's clan, shared among various persons in the clan. Marriage takes place in stages. Marriage is not finalised until the bride has born at least two children. When a third child is born, the marriage is considered "tied." At this point, the wife and the children become full members of the husband's clan. Women desire to have six children. A man may have multiple wives, who do not necessarily live close to each other. But they will all live in the area of the husband's clan.

Much more is common than different between the Nuer and the Dinka. They may share a common origin as related in a Nuer myth:

'God had two sons and promised his old cow to Dinka, and it's calf to Nuer. But Dinka went to God's cattle pen at night, imitating the voice of Nuer and thereby managing to get the calf. When God realised what happened, he was furious and urged Nuer to raid Dinka for cattle as revenge'. This is the state of affairs to date.

The similarities pose greater problems than the dissimilarities. Simply because the Dinka are so very much alike, they are the favourite war object of the Nuer. They can take wives and cattle to be assimilated into their clan. The problems with the Shilluk and other very dissimilar peoples are smaller, warfare being a rare event. In conflicts, it is the Nuer who by tradition takes the aggressive role.

Cattle among the Dinka are acquired as a gift from the father or relatives according to complicated rules. This gives the father and the elders an adamant position. Among the Nuer, cattle raiding from neighbouring non-Nuer is an accepted practice, even promoted among the young warriors. Apart from the social instability it creates, it also makes the position of the patriarch weaker than in Dinka society. Most conflicts involve cattle and the preponderance of Nuer customary law, like Dinka law, is taken up with cattle, feuds and family. In this respect, Dinka and Nuer customary law are very similar.

Shilluk

The Shilluk are the third and smallest group of Nilotic peoples of south Sudan. They are also uniquely different from the other two in that a king of divine origin rules them. The kingdom of Shilluk is located on the west bank of the Nile. Kingdom, mid-west Upper Nile covers a total area of 600 square miles. The Kingdom is bordered in the east and northeast by the White Nile and on the west by Western Upper Nile. Approximately 100,000 Shilluk live in the Kingdom.

Of the Nilotic people, the Shilluk are the most organised but less egalitarian. The four main clans surround their king, and some are entirely occupied in serving the king, to make the arrangements when he dies and the ceremonies following the installation of his successor. The clans with ceremonial duties live segregated from the "commoners".

The Shilluk have fewer cattle and are more sedentary than the Nuer and Dinka. They organise their societies along the riverside with each boundary running at right angles from the river. This makes for a variety of landscapes for each group: wet and dry gardens and grazing land. Fishing is critical and popular, and both sexes take part in the agricultural work. A community is commonly made of several hamlets with an elected headman. A council of the villages made up of the dominant lineage in the area elects the headman. Historically they were unified under one King or Reth chose from the sons of previous kings. Although closely related to the Dinka and Nuer [customary law] systems, Shilluk customary law is more orientated towards a hierarchical government with a single ruler and towards a more sedentary society with less emphasis on cattle as the key measure of wealth.

Zande

The Zande people (singular Azande) are a single ethnic group whose history centres on the geographic region of Western Equatorial, and the areas of the Democratic Republic of the Congo (DRC) and Central African Republic (CAR), which abut south Sudan. The Zande are agriculturalists with a history of conflict with other tribes, mainly the Dinka when they have attempted to farm cattle. They have a reputation for practising 'witchcraft' and other forms of mysticism. The Zande language is distinct to the people. The geography of their traditional tribal areas has exposed the Zande to external influences much more than other peoples and tribes of South Sudan. Consequently, they are more amenable to the forces of change and modernization. The Zande have mixed more readily with other smaller tribes in the region and their customs, practices and customary laws reflect the heterogeneous nature of their communities. Lacking cattle, their currency in customary law is principally money.

Fertit

The Fertit is a significant minority ethnic group with tribal areas in Western Bahr El Ghazal, centred on the two counties of Wau and Raja. Their communities are agriculturalist and sedentary. The Fertit are made up of some tribes, Balanda, Ndogo, Golo, Kreish, Yulu and Bongo. Their language is distinct, and their customs, practices and customary laws reflect their agriculturalist ethos. Like the Zande, the Fertit use money as the currency of customary law actions.

Anyuak

The Anyuak people are a single ethnic group with tribal areas in Eastern Upper Nile and southern Ethiopia. Their language is distinct and for many generations, they were cattle owners. The conflict between Anyuak and Nuer has resulted in the Anyuak turning to agriculture as a basis for their economy. Thus their customs, practices and customary laws reflect their agriculturalist lifestyle. The use of individual beads known as 'dimoi' as currency in common law issues, particularly 'bridewealth' is a unique feature of the Anyuak. The practice is in decline and money is more commonly used for such transactions.

Murle/Toposa

The Murle and Taposa are the larger and best known of a group of tribes, which inhabit Jonglei and eastern Equatorial. These tribes, comprising, Murle, Jie, Taposa, Boya, Didinga, Ngalam and Nyangatum are bound by geography, socio-economics (all are cattle-based societies) and language (though each has their dialect). The relationship between the tribes, particularly the Murle and Taposa has always been stormy. Conflict, invariably over cattle rustling, is a common state. The tribal areas are notorious for their disregard of 'government' whether British colonial, GOSS or SPLA/M. Moreover, frequent forays across the border into Kenya to steal cattle from the Turkana and their reputation for acts of banditry along the Kenyan/South Sudanese border, have earned the tribes and the region a reputation for lawlessness. The establishment of law and order in the region has been a priority for SPLA/M, and the establishment of their headquarters in Kapoeta County is a significant step in this process. These issues notwithstanding, there exists a strong system of customary law shared by the tribes, which has acted as an instrument for reconciliation between them and a means of communication and dialogue during the years of civil war.

Latuka/Pari /Acholi

These three are the major tribes of a tribal group which inhabits southeastern Equatoria and across the border into Uganda. Other tribes include Lokoya, Lango, Madi and Lopit. There are language differences, but a commonality of dialects provides a lingua franca for the communities. All are agriculturalists. Their customs and practices differ in some respects, but there are sufficient commonalities to provide a compatible system of customary laws.

Bari-Speaking

There are some tribes inhabiting the southern regions of Western Equatoria, bordering on DRC, which speaks a single language – Bari. They comprise the Bari, Pajulu, Kuku, Kakwa, Nyamgwara and Mundari. Their small size, common language and socio-economic status (all are agricultural communities) provide sufficient commonality of customs and practices to enable a compatible system of customary laws.

Maridi Ethnic Group

The counties of Maridi and Mundiri in Western Equatoria are also home to a group of tribes, classified by geographic region. They include the tribes of Moru, Mundu, Avokaya, Baka and Makaraka.

The tribes are agriculturalists and have a commonality of language with differing dialects. Their customs and practices allow for a compatible system of customary laws.

The below (figure 1) shows the breakdown of South Sudanese tribes :

1. Dinka (Main)
   Abiliang
   Agaar
   Aliab
   Atuot
   Bor
   Ciec
   Gok
   Hol
   Malual
   Nyarweng
   Padang
   Twic West
   Twic East
   Rek
   Ruweng

2. Nuer (Main)
   Adok
   Bul
   Garwaar
   Jegai
   Jikany
   Lek
   Lou
   Nyong

3. Anyuak
4. Jie
5. Adio
6. Aja
7. Ngalam (Kacipo)
8. Burum
9. Berta
10. Shilluk
11. Boya
12. Lopit
13. Pori
14. Latuka
15. Dindinga
16. Lango
17. Acholi
18. Lolubo
19. Madi
20. Murle/Toposa
11. Nyangatum
22. Lokoya
23. Bari
24. Pajulu
25. Baka
26. Kuku
27. Kakwa
28. Lubwara
29. Makaraka
30. Nyanwara
31. Mundari
32. Avokaya
33. Azande
34. Moru
35. Bongo
36. Jur bel
37. Jurchol -luo
38. Balanda Besia
39. Balanda Bagari
40. Fertit
41. Bingo
42. Kara
43. Keliku

44. Larim
45. shatt
46. Uduk
47. Tenet
48. Woro
49. Sere
50. Yulu
51. Pari
52. Nyangotom
53. Tid
54. Logir
55. Ifoto
56. Indri
57. Mananager
58. Ngulngule
59. Gollo
60. Kuka
61. Balanda -Boor
63. Dongotona
64. Feroghe
  Source: http://www.unocha.org/.

References

Mayardit, K. (K 2011). Presidential Speech at 1st Independence of South Sudan. *Presidential Speech at 1st Independence of South Sudan.*

(OCHA), O. f. (2013). http://www.unocha.org/.

Chapter Three
Ethnic group's role during wars of liberation

This chapter shall explore practical examples depicting prominent roles played by ethnic groups during the war. As in many wars, the role played by ethnic groups during the wars of liberation in Sudan could not be underrated. Indeed, the decades of a civil war of liberation in the old Sudan and subsequently in a recent past in South Sudan, have portrayed the enormous contribution of ethnic communities both collectively and as individual groups. The picture below shows the glimpse of how members of the civil population contributed to the war of liberation. Men voluntarily gave themselves whereas women provide food to the army.

During the war, men left villages to fight; women contributed food to the army.

Historically, the old Sudan that gave birth to the Republic of South Sudan has a rich history dating to thousands of years. Although Sudan was earlier occupied by native black African both in the north, west, east and south of the country, other foreigners navigated their ways to Sudan in about 2000 BC. For example, history has recorded that Ancient Egyptian traders sailed the Nile to Sudan (Rotberg 2008). These traders upon their arrival found native people (Nubians) in the extreme north of the country. The Nubians who had lived there for generations were subsistence farmers, herdsmen, and hunters. With enough crude African spirit of hospitality, these foreigners were received and entertained to share the resources of the land together with the natives. This hospitality was not reciprocated by the foreigners who indeed in about 1550 BC through Egypt invaded Sudan through the armies of the notorious Egyptian Pharaoh Ahmose. This army conquered the region of Kush and annexed it as the province of Egypt.

Despite this utter defeat, the Sudanese Nubians regrouped, reconsolidated like a ram that when defeated, typically pull back as a matter of tactics to gain momentum to hate back at a later stage with major force. Similarly, the Nubians regrouped back and restored their independence in about eleventh century B.C from the Egyptian invaders. History is replete with the facts that in about eight century B.C, the Nubians has conquered even the southern part of Egypt and had established the mighty kingdom of Kush in the city of Meroe on the Nile, north of modern Khartoum. As Kush army became stronger and most potent in the region, Egypt was not capable of pushing it back. However, in 30 B.C, Romans conquered Egypt and forced the Kush army back to Kush (Sudan), and subsequently the Roman army invaded North Sudan to stop Nubian raids into Egypt. The Romans continued to rule Sudan and Egypt and several other countries in the region for many years. Given, nature at the time, Romans went into a period of decline during the fourth to fifth centuries and left the country and the region.

By the seventh century, the black African in the Sudan confronted the new army; the Arab tribes, united by the fanaticism of their new religion of Prophet Mohamed. Post the death of their self-claim prophet who died in the 632, presumably the religious council resolved, to using force and other powers of persuasion in enforcing their religion. The African Nubians defeated the Arab army in 652, after that there was a peace agreement reached between the Arab tribes and the African. This peace accord lasted for decades and centuries.

This time of calm was exploited by the Arab tribes to networks, open business opportunities and indeed in this period, the Nubians sent slaves to Egypt in exchange for food and other essential commodities. In this period too, the Arabic language was taught, and Nubians agreed to it so as to make their business and communication easy on their sides. On the side of the Arab tribes, it was an opportunity to spread Islam and Arabization. As a result, the Nubian kingdom grew weaker and in 1276, the Mamluks, a powerful group of Muslim who ruled Egypt helped overthrow the king of Nubian kingdom and subsequently the region was converted to Islam. Christianity in this period faced a rapid decline.

Hence, by the end of 18th century, most of the modern Sudan was considered part of Egypt. Although, Sudan was regarded as part of Egypt, it was an independent entity but in 1820, the ruler of Egypt then, Muhammad Ali, invaded Sudan in the search of gold and other minerals wealth. In this war, over 50,000 Sudanese were killed, and 30,000 taken as slaves to Egypt. Historians have confirmed that this invasion marked 60 years of Egyptian rule over Sudan (Rotberg 2008). 1n 1899

Britain and Egypt put their acts together and agreed to share the control of Sudan.

This agreement was popularly known as Condominium, meaning "joint sovereignty by two nations." For the first half of the 20th Century, Sudan existed under the joint Anglo-Egyptian rule. Significantly, throughout this period the colonial administration chose to rule the vast country as though it were two distinct" ethnic groups – Arab Muslim North and a Black Christian/animists South. Although the demographic reality of Sudan was in fact far more mixed throughout, the colonial administration ruled according to this strict – and somewhat false – dichotomy.

Southern Sudan's remote and undeveloped provinces received "comparatively little official attention, except for sporadic attempts to suppress ethnic, tribal warfare, and the slave trade. The administration of the region occurred primarily through indirect rule, utilizing indigenous tribal chiefs" while at the same time virtually sealing the area off to the outside world by preventing trade with outsiders. At the same time, Christian missionaries operated a few schools and medical clinics, provided limited social services in Southern Sudan while encouraging Christianity among the region.

The emergence of first civil war in Sudan

Ten years before Sudan gained its independence, in 1956; the British decided to abandon the two distinct ruling policies for a single unified administration. However, this was done without consultation with Southern leaders, who by this stage had come to view their region as culturally, religiously and socio economically distinct from the North. Independence in 1956 was therefore heavily overshadowed by unresolved tensions with the South, which flared up into the full-scale civil war led by Anyanya, a rebel militant based in the South. On 18th August 1955, members of the British-administered Sudan Defense Force Equatorial Corps mutinied in Torit and the following days in Juba, Yei, and Maridi.

According to Joseph Lagu, the mutiny in Torit was not a planned rebellion although there were prior feelings of unease between southerners towards to the Arab north. The causes of mutiny in Torit were three-folds: firstly, the unfair trial of a southern politician in Khartoum. The southerners felt that their loved ones were mistreated and given an unfair trial. Secondly, an alleged leak of a telegram message giving northerners in the south a prerogative to mistreat southerners. Thirdly, the suspicious transfer of southern soldiers from Torit to Juba followed by the intention of disarming the soldiers and trucked them gun-less created more confusion and violence erupted. O'Ballance, writing in 1977, says that the 'period from 1955 to 1963 was simply one of guerilla survival, scarcely removed from banditry and that it was successful due to a score or so of former southern army officers and warrant officers, and a small number of non-commissioned civil servants'.

This first Sudanese internal civil war was mainly between the black African Southern Sudanese rebels and the northern Arab-led government. In the South, the rebellion named itself, the 'Anyanya' meaning "snake venom". The resistance believed that they were toxic to the north should the north refuse them their right to governance and economic prosperity. Indeed, as years of the war went 17 years) the Anyanya despite not having a proper weapon of war, were hideously poisonous to the political establishment in the north. The government in the north could not completely crush the rebels as alleged but opted for a negotiated settlement. This war took the lives of about 500,000 people from the South and North put together.

During the war, Col, Jaafar Nimeiry came to power by the military coup, in 1969. His rule was marked by many significant changes politically and economically. For example, he is on records, one among the top head of state to have outlawed political parties in the country. In other words Col. Jaafar deleted democracy in the country. Thus, the reaction of the suppressed political communities precipitated another military coup in 1971 although shortly Nimeiry was put back as Prime Minister by Communists. This practice was a lesson learned but quickly outlived.

In the South, as expected of any rebel movement, other changes were taking place. The late Aggrey Jaden was the leader but in a short while, mini-couped by Gordon Muortat. The coup against Aggrey was a setback as Aggrey's loyalists could not find reasons to support the Dinka-led army but fight with it. Again in 1971, former Lieutenant, Joseph Lagu took over from Gordon Muortat, this time under Joseph Lagu, the rebellion turned united, consolidated and triumphant to some extent. Joseph received support from the government of Israel.

Lagu managed to put together all pockets of the resistance under one solid command; and South Sudan Liberation Movement (SSLM) was then established. This establishment was then engaged by Khartoum in negotiating peace, and indeed that resulted in 1972 Addis Ababa Agreement.

Picture of General Joseph Lagu in South Sudanese bush fighting (1969).

Addis Ababa Agreement

Credit is given to the mediation between the World Council of Churches (WCC) and the All Africa Conference of Churches (AACC), both of which spent years building up trust with the two combatants, eventually led to the Addis Ababa Agreement of March 1972 ending the conflict (Assefa 1987) in which the then military-led government of President Nimeiri agreed to political autonomy – though not full independence – for the South, and with that the Anyanya rebellion died down.

When asked as to what guarantees were in place for the implementation of protocols in the 1972 Addis Ababa Agreement. General Joseph Lagu who once led Anyanya One Rebellion, in his 2012 SSTV interview stated categorically that, there were no tangible guarantees for the implementation of Addis-Abba Agreement but he allowed it for the following reasons: Firstly, many South Sudanese in the form of civil organizations had requested him through many letters and scripts to sign the agreement and bring southerners back. Joseph thought if this was the public opinion of Southern Sudanese, then there was no need to reject the people's call for peace.

Secondly, Anyanya Rebellion at the time had lost a key ally which was Uganda. President Amin Dada had turned against the Anyanya and was collaborating with Khartoum and the Arab world. Thus, Joseph saw the possibility of his officers including his real self-being surrendered by President Amin to Khartoum. Thirdly, the momentum and resources to continue fighting the war were diminishing, strategically; the rebellion was at the edge of defeat. Conditionally, Joseph and his team accepted the 1972 agreement as a pull back to gain momentum with a possible return to the bush at a later given stage. Therefore, in exchange for ending their armed uprising, southerners were granted a single southern administrative region with various defined powers.

However, this agreement was denounced as a sellout by former leaders Aggrey Jaden and Gordon Muortat Mayen. The agreement's demise was predicted by both, with Muortat going on to form and lead the African National Front, an opposition movement against the Addis Ababa talks and agreement. The picture shows two southern Sudanese negotiators holding hands witnessed by Emperor Haile Selassie of Ethiopia

Abel Alier (Rep Khartoum), General Lagu (Rep Anyanya Movement
Source: http://www.selassiestandup.org/?q=node/3

The emergence of second civil war

In September 1982, as part of the Islamicization of the country, President Nimeiri declared his intention to incorporate extreme elements of Islamic Shari'a law in the penal code. These laws made life harder for non-Muslims in the country and many southerners, in particular, were bruised by these laws. Without any exaggeration, these conditions among other issues including intended marginalization led to the speedy resumption of civil war. John Garang who was Col in the Army at the time, and his southern colleagues risked their lives to rebel against the well-resourced government Philosophically, Southerners were motivated by the truth of being owners of the land of South Sudan in particular. They maneuvered to gain support from some African Countries. Although the rebels had no pay during the war, they presented a threat to the regime in Khartoum, which conditioned changes in the north. For example:

> "In 1985, after widespread popular unrest Nimieri was removed from power by a group of officers and a Transitional Military Council was established to rule the country. A year later a coalition government was formed after general elections, with Sadiq al-Mahdi as Prime Minister.
>
> See more on the website below (www.insightonconflict.org/conflicts/sudan/conflict-profile/)."

The Sudanese People Liberation Army (SPLA) continued with the civil war, recruiting and training members; both conscripted and those who voluntarily presented themselves to the training camps. The SPLA prepared these civilians for the battles that lasted for 21 years before peace settlement was initially reached. In these battles, millions of people lost their lives, millions got displaced, exiled such as myself, unaccounted properties and animals destroyed in unimaginable proportion. In both the first and second wars in the Sudan, South Sudanese fought along with their ethnic group-battalions and camps. The tribe's communities were used firstly as recruiting sources for militants, conscripting able young people into the army training camps.

The armed rebellions were seen as rebellion against persecutions, slavery and forceful taking of people's land and resources. Secondly, tribe-communities provided logistics and other essential services to the army in trenches and military camps. Dr. John Garang in one of his frequent briefing after the comprehensive peace agreement, acknowledged this, and I, quote, "during the protracted civil wars in the Sudan, we the SPLA used our civilian population as our logistics, they provided us food and other war needed necessities (Garang's briefing on CPA 2004).

In the same presentation, Dr. Garang concluded by thanking the civil population for their valuable contributions to the war of liberation during the tedious 21 years of confrontation with Khartoum Regimes. In another speech made to the army, Garang used the illustration of a river with water and fishes. He compared that soldiers are like fishes who cannot survive if not in the water. Contextually, he equated civil population with water on which the fish lifeline is base; he asserted that soldiers must respect and live with the civilian population in harmony.

Rebellions within Rebellion

John Garang is praised as charismatic rebel leader that fought and endured numerous internal rebellions in the Movement and remained victorious to the very end. Although the resistance within the Movement reached a critical point to the near demise of the SPLM/A, John Garang in his wisdom prevails many attempts by the enemies of peace and unity of the marginalized people of Sudan. He resisted enemies who had wanted to destroy the Movement and John Garang himself as well. Dr. Adwok Nyaba, in his book, The Politics of Liberation in South Sudan, clarifies:

> "It is rare that a liberation movement takes off and achieves its objectives or comes to power without having passed through the tunnel of contractions, in-fighting and perhaps splits (Nyaba 2000, p.135)."

This assertion is true of the Sudan People Liberation Movement (SPLM/A). Although SPLM/A was a people-based revolution in its original nature, it nevertheless went through some significant contractions. Right from the inception in 1983, the movement was faced with internal rebellion between Anya Nya 2 headed by Hon Akuot Atem and Gai Tut plus their followers and Elite group led by Dr. John Garang, including William Nyuon Bany, Kerbino Kuanyin Bol, and their supporters. Primarily, this rebellion was caused by what I could call a leadership ambition, coupled with the lack of a comprehensive vision of liberation.

The two groups parted ways and became enemies to each other. Good enough, this was not essentially a tribal conflict; otherwise people like Hon Akuot Atem Mayen would not have left his distance cousin John Garang from a Dinka Bor tribe and joined Gai Tut from a Nuer tribe. But as rebellions go, there are always contradictions. Anya Nya 2 later became a pure Nuer tribe movement, and Hon Akuot Atem, a Dinka man from Bor, was assassinated in cold blood in the Nuer land.

However, SPLM/A under able John Garang flourished after having cleared Anya Nya 2 rebellion. The Movement grew popular and successful in its initial years, capturing garrison towns from the Sudan government. Thousands of marginalized Sudanese joined the movement from all corners of the country, predominantly from Southern Sudan, Nuba Mountains from the far north and later on members of the Darfur from the western part of the country, also joined. The Movement then changed its focus and became a National Movement with the vision of New Sudan of equality, democratic transformation and justice for all irrespective of their race, ethnicity and religion.

As earlier stated by Dr. Adwok Nyaba, SPLM/A was rocked by internal rebellion on August 28th, 1991 speared by Dr. Riek Machar and Dr. Lam Akol plus their followers. Dr. Adwok wrote brief narrative about the second internal rebellion of 1991, here below he saw how this revolution unfolded;

> August 28th, 1991 will go down in the history of South Sudan as the most important single day when the people of South Sudan's aspiration for freedom and justice suffered a severe blow at the hands of its sons. The Movement's weakest moment was turned into an incentive for power struggle by some of its ablest sons. It was a power struggle that was driven by wishful thinking and possible encouragement by the enemy rather than meticulous political and social engineering. The radio message of Dr. Riek Machar to all SPLA units was done without prior knowledge or consent of the targeted groups. It was made in the 'hope' that those dissatisfied with Garang's leadership would join and support the coup (I bid p 89).

This rebellion resulted in a big battle of the SPLM/A fighting itself; those soldiers who deserted with Riek and those loyal to Dr. John Garang. Thousands of lives were lost in the war between the rebellion under Riek Machar and the loyalists of Dr. John Garang. The objective of Riek-Lam coup and war of 1991 was mainly to overtake Dr John Garang whom they accused of dictatorial tendencies and reconstitute democratic SPLM/A. When asked on the accusation of authoritarian tendency directed to him from the camp of Dr. Riek Machar, Garang reiterated that he was not leading any government. They are instead fighting to take over the government in

Khartoum, and he accused the Riek's camp of short-sightedness for demanding a government from him which is conventional nonexistence.

On the question of dictatorial tendencies directed to him, Garang affirmed that SPLM/A was a tool to bring about democracy and that a tool cannot be democratic! He stated that they can only disagree with each other and that each of them has to detour to any part of the bushes. Although 1991 was a major rebellion, other minor rebellions ensued, and Garang through all these remained unwavered until the very end, where he negotiated the comprehensive peace agreement in 2005.

Comprehensive Peace Agreement, 2005

Many peace talks preceded the comprehensive peace agreements. The majority of the peace negotiations died in infancy, some talks was signed in the quest of ending the Sudanese conflict. Surprisingly, the majority of those signed treaties have not been implemented and honored, as testified by as Hon Uncle Abel Alier in his book entitled: *Many agreements dishonored*. Despite these routines of disrespect of signed treaties, the comprehensive peace agreement was above all others exceptional. The uniqueness of the 2005 Comprehensive Peace Agreement (CPA) was its provision that gave South Sudan the right of self-determination within the period of six years. Indeed, Southerners were provided with the opportunity after the interim period of six years to vote to remain as part of Sudan or opt to be a separate country. Hence, it is a known fact that:

> Comprehensive Peace Agreement (CPA) was signed by the political wing of the SPLA, the SPLM (Sudan Peoples' Liberation Movement) and Omar al-Bashir's National Congress Party (NCP) in Khartoum, bringing an official end to the war. By the CPA, a referendum was to be held on 9 January 2011 to determine whether the South should remain part of Sudan or become independent while in the six intervening years the South was given the opportunity to begin building the foundations of its government.
> See more on the website below (www.insightonconflict.org/conflicts/sudan/conflict)

When right time was bestowed to Southerners in 2011, they overwhelmingly voted, approximately 98%, for the separation of the country and chose to opt for an independent South Sudan. The internationally monitored referendum was conducted, and the result affirmed the separation of South Sudan and it was unanimous. Joyfully, on the 9th July 2011, South Sudan was recognized as an independent country. The 193rd Country in the world of nations with her flag installed on the high ground on the world stage.

Concurrently, a similar referendum was expected to be held in the disputed border region of Abyei to decide whether it joined the North or South, but this has been postponed due to a failure to reach agreement on the terms of the referendum. These days, Sudan, in some scripts, is referred as a country in North Africa, sometimes considered part of the Middle East perhaps politically. However, the Republic of South Sudan is now part of East Africa. Although Sudan and South Sudan have parted ways, the two countries are still bound together by many things including the language (Arabic), culture, and more importantly oil pipeline through which Southern oil is transported through to Port Sudan.

References

Alier, A. (1990.). *Southern Sudan: Too many agreements dishonored.* New York: : Ithaca Press.

Assefa, H. T. (1987). Mediation of Civil Wars, Approaches and Strategies-the Sudan Conflict. *Westview Press. Colorado:.*

Eprile, C. (1974.). *War and Peace in the Sudan, 1955 – 1972.* London: David and Charles.

Garang, J 2004 Dr Garang public briefing on machakos protocols

Johnson, D. H. (1979). "Book Review: The Secret War in the Sudan: 1955–1972 by Edgar O'Ballance". *African Affairs*, (310):132–7.

Lagu, J. (2006). *Sudan: Odyssey through a State (From Ruin to Hope.* Taylor and Francis Ltd.

(n.d.). *First Sudanese Civil war.* http://www.absoluteastronomy.com/topics/First_Sudanese_Civil_War

(n.d.). *Sudanese civil war.* http://mapyourinfo.com/wiki/en.wikipedia.org/the%3DFirst%3DSudanese%3DCivil%3.

(n.d.). *Centre for alternative discourse manipur.* http://cad-manipur.org/in-focus/.

(n.d.). *Sudan conflict .* http://www.insightonconflict.org/conflicts/sudan/conflict-profile/.

(n.d.). *Sudan history.* http://www.anasudani.net/english-5.html.

Nyaba, P.A 2000 *Politics of liberation in South Sudan: An insider's view* Kampala: Fountain publishers ltd

O'Ballance, E. (1977). *The Secret War in the Sudan: 1955–1972.* Hamden,: Connecticut: Archon Book.

(O'Ballance, 1. S. (1999.). *War and Conflict in Southern Sudan, 1955–1972. PhD Dissertation,,.* Santa Barbara.: University of California.

Chapter Four
Negative ethnic politics

Ethnic groups in Sudan have contributed enormously to the war efforts as discussed in the previous chapter. They (ethnic groups) have, however, in recent decades, proven as an incredible source of conflicts or have been used to wage battles. The common reason is that these ethnic groups are tribalized, and thus tribalism has taken its full course on the innocent citizens. This chapter shall explore practical examples of tribally and ethnically engineered conflicts in South Sudan. The chapter shall, however, attempt to amalgamate views of a few citizens who stand against tribalism, narrate on how such views could contribute to future de-ethnicization of South Sudan politics.

As this analysis proceeds, it is relevant to define the interlocking term (tribalism), so as to understand the features its entails. Tribalism is " the behavior and attitudes that stem from strong loyalty to one's tribe or social group".... it may also refer in "cultural terms to a way of thinking or behaving in which people are more loyal to their tribe than to their friends, their country, or any other social group (en.wikipedia.org/wiki/Tribalism)"

Also, Youth against Tribalism in Africa (YATIA) defined tribalism as "the discrimination and animosities caused by tribal groups to each other that create social, economic, physical, emotional, and religious sabotage within their society

(See YATIA web page)." Similarly in Namibia, they defined a tribe as "a grouping of people whose loyalty to their group is greater than their loyalty to a nation. Gerson argues, "It is against this background that tribalism should not be allowed to rear its ugly head in our beautiful country, Namibia (Gerson 2008)." The prevailing realities in South Sudan reflected these definitions and defined the ongoing South Sudanese conflicts.

The Country is severely divided into ethnic lines. It is not surprising to know that South Sudanese live as divided people with divided loyalties. These parallel commitments have facilitated conflicts among South Sudanese. Francis Mading in his book entitled Self-Determination and National Unity: a challenge for Africa, stressed that most of the African conflicts have their roots in mismanaged diversity. He emphasized that most governments in Africa don't appear inclusive in governance, such non-inclusiveness precipitate much of the existing conflicts in Africa (Deng 2010, p.12). In Francis Deng's views, it is critical to see how Africans abuse a reality that is cultural diversity that has and continue to exist for generations. The notion that the continent is naturally multiethnic begs acceptance from the policy makers in a public institution.

However, these days within South Sudanese political and social circles, it is worth mentioning that a common identity (being South Sudanese) is fading away. It is ethnic grouping that is being given the attention. Hence, it is rather shocking to see a vast nation being disintegrated by her products (people). Thus it is perceivable that even God is begging us, the South Sudanese to stop dissolving this beautiful society. I am, like many other South Sudanese, worried by seeing nothing positive each day on the expected walking steps toward unifying ethnic groups, putting more efforts on national healing and reconciliation.

It is heartening to see tribal segments glorified in the national television broadcaster, especially from prominent public servants. In recent years and during 2013 conflicts, the media was dominated by the vicious war of words coated in ethnic flavors, targeting ethnic groups and elements. For example, the utterances projected by newly formulated traditional tools such as the so-call Jieng Council of Elders, Equatoria Council of Rights, the Nuer Council. Fervently, these councils only play tribal politics, and indeed through these councils, important things such as the national identity are lost. Honestly, these councils represent the Stone Age politics of tribal groups' competition against each other.

Many among you will agree with me that nice setup in Africa is glued up in the notion of tribes. The people that you relate with in most parts of your life are your tribe men and women, and as a young child, you only grew among your tribe people. Speaking the very same language, dance the same tune; eat the same type of food, and more importantly share the same environment. Scientifically and anthropologically, one world view is shaped by this knowledge-ability.

Thus, it is not a surprise to hear the utterances of this world view being penetrated into the system of governance in the country. As government makes decisions presumably based on merit and connection, such as the appointment of officials. People of such world-views would start speculating after seeing none of their tribe' person appointed, that the nomination was tribalistic. The question would be: who is tribalistic here? It is the one thinking that his or her tribe men must be appointed? Or one who selected people with which to him or her is based on merit? Obviously, the tribalistic person is one that thinks that any appointment must come from his or her proximity in terms of his or her tribe men or women.

The government in both developed and developing countries will never work that way. The government will never be based on tribes; it is a tribe less institution that is guided both by general laws and international practice. This is contrary to how our people in South Sudan think; in fact the majority of people have developed this uninformed concept of tribalism. They criticize every steps that President, His Excellency General Salva Kiir Mayardit undertakes.

Some went as far as saying that the appointments he makes are tribally guided. To me it is an absolute lie; the President has several advisors plus his own true wisdom. With this strong stance, how and where can tribalism come in? Ironically, when a capable Dinka person is appointed, as Kiir is naturally a Dinka, does that constitute tribalism? How do you separate capabilities and the ability to do things from the so-called tribal appointment?

This leads me to shed light on the notion of majority vs. minority. Of course in every country in Africa, there are majority tribes and minor tribes. In Kenya the Kikuyu are a majority followed by the Luyah. In South Sudan, Dinka is a majority tribe followed by the Nuer and the rest are minorities. It is this set up that sometimes precipitates talk of tribalism. However, Dr. Garang once said, "There is no body's majority and minority…" he was right to say that, indeed there are no such things as majority tribes in government.

The notion of the majority that people talk about in government is the majority in political parties. For example in South Sudan, SPLM is a majority party. It can win the elections by a high margin or have laws passed unanimously. Parties recruit members' based on their policies and vision. A minority party is one that lacks vision or is poor in selling its policies and vision to the masses. If there is tribalism in South Sudan, where does it come from? And who is being targeted? Apparently, they say that 'what goes around comes around,' indeed there are always voices of complaints from minority groups. These groups think that they are left out in the formation of the government, or their rights are being compromised by those in power.

There may be some elements of truth in this but overall if a complaint comes from Kuku for example that their numbers do not match with Nuer in the government let say number of MPs. The question then becomes, how can that be realistic? How many counties are in Nuer land compared with counties in Kuku land for example? How many constituencies in Kuku land vs. Nuer? How many States in South Sudan are Nuer situated and how many States are Kuku? Arithmetically, the match between Nuer tribe and kuku tribe in this context will never work. If this is the level of talk about tribalism, then it is baseless and must not be encouraged.

Readers, I am convinced that the continuing discussions on perceived tribalism will take us to absolutely nowhere but will only promote tribal hatred. Let us allow the government of the day to assemble ministries with personnel they believe that they fit the set criteria. Let us be nationalist and look at capabilities. I have no problem with all Anuak MPs being made ministers as long as they are capable of articulating development projects in their respective ministries.

The picture below portrays dark spots on the Dinka and Nuer future relationship. It illustrates how Dinka and Nuer civilians were separated during conflicts in 2013.
Source: http://www.selassiestandup.org/?q=node/3

Theories underpinning Tribalism and conflicts

As stated by Francis Deng above, most of the ongoing conflicts in South Sudan have their roots and origins from glorifying ethnic groups at the expense of other ethnic entities and thus compromising national identity. In this relation, some theories underpinning this belief have emerged. One of these is the belief that the South Sudanese have no experience of ownership of a nationality or a shared common identity. All they (South Sudanese) know are their tribal groups and nearby neighbors. This theory gives the impression that most conflicts shall continue until the time that South Sudanese learn and appreciate their shared identity.

In conformity with this opinion, Dr. Hassan al-Turabi, when asked in the wake of 2013 Juba conflict, why the South Sudanese resumed brutal internal conflict among themselves, Dr Hassan replied that "South Sudanese never had any collective identity; they were brought together and seen solidly together only during the referendum campaign, because they had one agenda, to vote for an Independent South Sudan, which they correctly did, but when that ended, South Sudanese went back to their tribal groups (Dr. Hassan El Turabi, interview, 2013)." This view is held by many people in the old Sudan and presumably by some objective South Sudanese.

The second theory speculates that the South Sudanese grew up with some fallacies against each other tribes. One example of this; some individuals in some tribes believes that they were born to rule others and that their tribe is the best! These categories of people don't want see anybody to be made a national leader unless he or she is from their tribe. They are the so-called; 'White Army', 'Duku Beny' (which literally means 'reach to rescue the president) also known as Mathiang Ayoor in that matter, 'Equatoria Defense Force,' Shilluk Militias, Murle raiders among others and Etc.

As a matter of fact, these categories of people have no regards for nationalism. For example, when one leader of the so-called white army was asked to explain how they would wish to have the conflict ended, He replied, "the conflict will only end when Dr. Riek Machar is being installed as president of the Republic of South Sudan, full stop." In similar moderation, personnel of Duku Beny also known as mathiang Ayoor believed that President Kiir will only be unseated over their dead bodies. Also seen in recent peace talks, are the governors of the Greater Equatoria, grouped together around protecting the position of Vice President Hon Wani Igga, they argued that Wani, the son of their region must not be stepped less than the position he holds whatsoever the case may be. In other words, the governors are happier to have Hon Wani as Vice President, instead of having peace with Wani in the third position.

Conventionally, this is a serious contradiction to typical institutional protocol for the following reasons: First, the governors of the so-called Greater Equatoria are already represented by SPLM delegation to Addis Ababa peace talks; they are too represented by President Kiir, and there is no reason to present a parallel position in the same peace talk by the same institution (SPLM). Secondly, it appears that the governors have impulsively undermined the officially delegated team to the peace talks, or they expressed no trust on the SPLM negotiating team. Seemingly these rulers took a silence vote of no confidence both in the SPLM negotiating team and presumably on the sitting president.

Equivocally, the above theories explained the rationale necessitating why such unconventional confused utterances continue to occur in the Republic of South Sudan. The theories depict the root causes of most if not all of the past and present conflicts in South Sudan. Clearly, there is an enormous gap between loyalties; that is between loyalty to one's tribe group and that to the nation. Presumably, South Sudanese are more loyal and pay much allegiance to their tribes and communities than they are to the nation.

This, too, explained why nepotism and corruption are common in all public institutions in South Sudan. People get the job through their relatives in senior positions, making those individuals without significant weights in critical public institutions, vulnerable people though with high qualifications. Such practice has accelerated South Sudan although as two years old to join the top world failed state as well as one of the top corrupt countries in the world. Few objective South Sudanese are only left to agonize in the less rescuing situation. A South Sudanese well-known commentator, Zechariah Manyok Biar in his article published on 14th May 2014, in the distinguished website call Sudantribune.com, painted the picture of this image clearly, he said:

> Since South Sudanese only knew tribes and tribal leaderships, they feel uncomfortable today to do anything that does not take into account the tribal loyalty. That is why it is difficult for anybody. However, fair-minded he or she is, to stand in the middle and do justice in addressing issues of national importance. Those who stand in the midst of our current setting do not get anything better than being trampled upon by both

their communities and the diverse communities. It is seen as strange for anybody to criticize his or her community and be criticized by its members. Those who attempt to criticize their communities are seen as traitors. So, we keep siding with our communities in everything to avoid being seen as traitors. Because we do not know anything better than our tribes, we associate individual happiness and security to our tribes since, not doing so would be naïve. We fear the unknown in other communities because there is no way of knowing them better. As a result, we stick to our own in everything, ranging from marriage to politics. Our myopia convinces each tribe that it is the only best tribe in the country. That is why we coin derogatory names to refer to others such as Door, Jenge, Nyagat, Bheer, Nyamnyam, among others. We glory in things that do not matter even at the national level because we subordinate the state to tribes and not the other way around. Distorted beliefs of each tribe are practiced in national offices today in South Sudan, making unity in diversity difficult (Zechariah Manyok Biar, 2013 www.sudantribune.com/spip.php?article51002).

In the above article, Mr. Biar believes that those holding leadership positions in South Sudan, of various political parties and institutions, have contributed to negative ethnic politics through encouraging tribal utterances in the public sphere. For example, many South Sudanese politicians crown themselves with their tribe men and women; they only feel secure when surrounded by the tribe folks of their own.

This practice thus shaded and continued to wipe away national identity, giving birth to only tribal hatred, enmity and the notion of encroaching into avenues of national disintegration. Such unlevelled ground produced many forms and circle of violence. Few examples of these are: Firstly, the 1991 rebellion within SPLM/SPLA which turned obnoxiously tribal, and many people on tribal line were killed, maimed and mercilessly massacred in cool blood. Dr. Riek's army of predominantly of Nuer ethnic background with civilian elements of Nuer civilians launched ethnic cleansing on the people of Duk, Twic, and Bor counties, killing civilians, children, women and abducting others.

The entire region referred by some people in contemporary writing as greater Bor was reduced to ashes. The cattle were taken, and thousands of people displaced from their homes and villages. Dr. Riek instead of fighting Dr. Garang's army in their trenches and bushes launched ethnic targeting war against Eastern Dinka of Jonglei. On the other hands, unverified records presumably from oral source have portrayed how Nuer ethnic groups were once targeted by Dinka soldiers of Dr. Garang in the pretext of Nuer as being people known for rebellion turns (nyagat). Stories of massacred by soldiers loyal to then Dr. Garang are replete in the nuer communities. Stories are told how soldiers could put families into luak and burn it down with people including women and children. Secondly, cattle raiding between tribes and communities have continued to generate most of the tribal conflict in South Sudan.

Cattle have been a primary source of communal conflict in recent years. Unlike old days, raids in the last few years have been deadly given the facts that there are guns at the hands of raiders. In some cultures, cattle raiding are part of young people traditional initiation, in such communities young men must go and attack animals somewhere to mark their manhood in the community. In other communities, cattle's raiding's conducted for purely economic gained. Animals are used as dowries in marriages, and they are also used for food regarding milk and meat. Although fingers are pointed to particular ethnic groups who's the notion of cattle raiding is believed to be their traditional practice.

Other tribes in a recent past have practiced the vice altogether. It thus becomes a national problem in the country where the civil population is severely militarized. The figure two (2) below shows the simple matrix of ethnically-based cattle raiding, especially in rural villages and cattle camps. The two-way arrows indicate that the two communities pointed by arrow, raids each other.

Figure 2: Tribe to tribe Cattle Raidings		
Murle	←——→	Dinka
Shilluk	←——→	Nuer
Murle	←——→	Nuer
Toposa	←——→	Tarkana(Kenya)
Murle	←——→	Anyuak
Mundari	←——→	Dinka
Dinka	←——→	Mundari

Thirdly, abduction of children from parents continues to be a rampant practice in South Sudan primarily practiced by individual communities. Globally, child abduction is stated as child theft, or unconsented taking away of children from their parents or careers. Predominantly in western countries such as Australia, the term child abduction conflates two legal and social categories that differ in their perpetrating contexts that are (a) kidnapping by members of the child's family or (b) abduction by strangers.

In South Sudan, most of these abduction types are not applicable. For example, unlike The US and another civilized world, kidnapping in South Sudan is done mainly by first communities. They don't sell children or use them for sexual exploitation, or slavery, and human trafficking. However, most of the children abducted in South Sudan ended up being adopted by parents with no or fewer children. They are taken care of as their children and in some cases some of these children later leaked their origin and they voluntarily returned to their original homes. South Sudan does have law against the abduction of children; the common dialog is used to negotiate the return of abducted children. This approach has not been successful regarding stopping the vice of child abduction in these rural villages and the country as a whole. The practice is continuing even now; children continue to be abducted, and parents continue to suffer the anguish of their loved children.

Political ethnically motivated conflict

"If you succumb to the temptation of using violence in the struggle, unborn generations will be the recipients of a long and wild night of bitterness and your chief legacy to the future will be an endless reign of meaningless chaos (Martin Luther King, Jr)"

As it came to be widely known, the 14 December 2013 was the time when the SPLM political elites (two organs namely Political Bureau (PB) National Liberation Council (NLC) hosted a meeting that later precipitated shootings resulting in the public unrest. Few members of these organs are on record to have walked out in the meeting citing dictatorial tendencies. They came out criticizing the strengthening of authoritarian tendencies, lack of collective and democratic decision-making opportunities. Unfortunately, as briefly stated above, the black Sunday of December 15th, 2013 was triggered by the deficiency of political will to compromise and forge ahead with United SPLM Party.

Picture of SPLM leaders who hosted press conference on Dec 6 2013, calling for reforms in the SPLM.
First left (Pagan), left (Nyandeng), centre Dr Riek, next Deng Aloor, Lado Gore, extreme right Taban Deng Gai
Source :(www.sudnatribune.com-500x256)

The ticking bomb was left to explode, and that indeed happened on what is now referred to as Black Sunday the 15th December 2013. With unlevelled ethnic hatred already bred, both members of ethnic groups during these conflicts saw themselves obliged to kill each other in the name of protecting their tribe, properties, and men in high-ranking positions whom they think must not be touched. Realistically, the violence has its origins in a stand-off between different factions of the presidential guards.

Hirblinger observed, "this fault-line quickly spread within the armed forces, as the fighting over key strategic locations in Juba pitched members of the Dinka and Nuer ethnic groups against each other. Reports of targeted killings and perpetrators selecting victims based on their association with particular ethnic groups suggest that distinctions between friends, enemies, and various combat strategies were widely informed by the framework of ethnic belonging (Ibid)."

In the midst of this confusion, local South Sudanese and international commentators in the persons of: Andreas Hirblinger, Hannah Bryce, Magai Mayuon, late Isaiah Abraham, Kuir Garang, Zechariah Manyok Biar (whom I quoted earlier) Thon Agany, among others, have written a detailed articles on political and ethnically motivated conflicts in the world newest country, South Sudan.

Equally, there are a wide range of written opinion articles and analysis by these individuals and myself. I, fully acknowledge their great works in bringing to light issues of significance to the consumption of the next generation of South Sudanese. In the first instant, Andreas Hirblinger has argued that "the use of ethnicity as a frame of reference in the resurgent armed conflict stands in contrast to the much more subtle and complex role of communal belonging in South Sudan's mainstream politics (Hirblinger 2013)." He concluded, "threat of ethnic conflict is used by both sides in all conflicts that have occurred in South Sudan as a strategy to legitimize the crackdown on the alleged perpetrators of violence (Ibid)." Hannah Bryce (2013) in her article entitle: The Dangers of Tribalism in South Sudan, argues:

The dynamics of the leadership struggle between President Salva Kiir, a Dinka, and former vice president Riek Macher, a Nuer, colours politics throughout the country, illustrating the prevalence of political tribalism at the highest office. Following Kiir's dismissal of Machar and the entire cabinet in July, neither this week's attempted coup nor its heavy suppression will have come as a surprise to many in South Sudan.

The perception of Dinka domination pervading the Sudan People Liberation Movement (SPLM) and the Sudan People Liberation Army (SPLA) by other ethnic groups is not new. But it has become increasingly marked in a country with a fragile economy, limited opportunities for employment and deep-rooted patrimonialism throughout all tiers of government. While there is a long-standing rivalry for power between the Dinka and Nuer, South Sudan's two largest tribal groups, others, such as the Equatorians, perceive both groups as monopolizing power. Addressing this perceived inequity within the government will be integral to move beyond political tribalism towards an inclusive system of government that guarantees minority representation.

Without this change, discontent and frustrations within the disenfranchised rural communities that make up the majority of the population are liable to rise to the surface (Bryce 2013).

Furthermore, Thon Agany Ayiei, a columnist for The New Sudan Vision, paraded contemporary historical accounts of Dink-Nuer conflicts.

In his analysis, Ayiei suggested multiple causes of Dinka- Nuer conflicts, especially in the modern times. Interestingly, Dinka and Nuer are believed to have descended from one mother and father, over millions of years ago. This theory is supported by the facts that Dinka and Nuer shared similar cultures and traditions.

These two communities intermarried more than any other communities. For example, close to the time of conflict eruption in Juba, a successful intermarriage was done between a young boy from Dinka (Mr. Biar Ajak Deng from Jonglei state) and a young girl from Nuer (Ms. Nyanthon Hoth Mai from Upper State). This marriage brought together key leaders of the two big tribes (Dinka & Nuer). Dr. Riek Machar was the elder handing over Nyanthon Hoth Mai, and late Uncle Elijah Malok Aleng was an elder receiving the girl. Indeed, it was a joyous ceremony for the two communities.

Fascinating cultural values were exchanged and edified. Agany (2013) in his article entitled "Understanding the tribal, political and economic aspects of the current South Sudan civil war and their complications in achieving a peaceful, lasting solution," stated that Dinka and Nuer

> "Are of Nilotic origin, characterized by their physical features of being dark and tall. Their livelihood largely depends on cattle and subsistence farming. Between December and January, their water sources around their permanent establishments dry up, and they are forced to move to the swarm areas along the River Nile. Their second movement is between May and June when they return to their permanent estates as the rains start to fall. Therefore, in many aspects, Dinka and Nuer are brothers who can only be distinguished by language and traditional markings. In fact, Dinkas who directly share the border with Nuers such as the Hol in Duk Padiet, Nyarweng in Duk Pawuel, most of Dinka Ngok and some Dinka Bar El Ghazal share the same traditional marks and speak each other's languages."
> Source: http://www.newsudanvision.com/sudan/2813-

As expected from most of the countries, neighboring tribes in Africa, the Dinka and Nuer have their border issues. There are many minor issues causing skirmishes between the frontier of both Dinkas and Nuers, but cattle raiding and competition for water and pastures around the swarm areas are known to be the primary causes of their major border conflicts (understanding the tribal, 2015). However, in recent years Dinka and Nuer have been collided by politicians and military personnel in what I would call contemporary conflict. I must acknowledge that these contemporary conflicts have caused thousands of lives between these communities.

In comparison, the causalities caught in these conflicts have exceeded those exterminated during the olden days of spears- wars. Self-explanatorily, the modern weapons involved in recent conflicts have carried the load that destroys lives in a macro sense.

The sophistication of the war machines in the 21st century has unfortunately taken a toll on the Dinka and Nuer communities. The figure below shows timelines of such contemporary political engineered conflicts. The figure below shows schedules of such political engineered conflicts.

Figure 3: Dinka and Nuer Contemporary political conflicts

Conflict actors	Purpose and extent of conflicts
1984 Garang vs Gai Tut	Both leaders, were fighting for South Sudanese freedom, they disagreed on an ideological basis. Gai was then killed; Akuot a Dinka, who was together with Gai Tut, was killed by Nuer mourners. William Abdallah Chuol seized control of Gai Tut's forces who were almost entirely Nuer to carry on the fight against John Garang's forces. This fighting did not have any significant impact on civilians as the two armies confined their fighting to fighting only the armed elements of their forces.
1991 Garang vs Riek	The second political disagreement that resulted in a fight that pitted the Dinka against Nuer came in 1991 when Dr. Riek Machar Teny, a Nuer military General rebelled against his Dinka Commander in Chief, Dr. John Garang. As the disagreement between Gai Tut and John Garang in 1984, Machar disagreement with John Garang was based on ideological differences with Machar opting for the full separation of South Sudan from Sudan, while John Garang maintained his vision of fighting for a unified new Sudan.
	Again, the political disagreement between Machar and Garang quickly developed into a tribal war between Dinka and Nuer. Unlike the 1984 war that was mainly confined to the two armed factions, the 1991 war was an all-out war that resulted in the untold suffering of civilians on both sides, although the Dinka civilians suffered at much greater scale than the Nuers.

2013 kiir vs Riek	In July 2013, President Salva Kiir sacked his Vice President, Dr. Machar and dissolved the entire Cabinet and appointed new Cabinet Ministers. On December 6, 2013, Dr. Machar and a group of former government officials relieved with him months earlier held a press conference in the Capital Juba in which they demanded reforms in the ruling party, the SPLM. Nine days later, on December 15th, a fight broke out in Juba that quickly spread to the rest of the country. After a day of fighting in Juba, Machar and his armed supporters left Juba and headed to Bor were the Sudan People's Liberation Army (SPLA) Division 8 under Major General Peter Gatdet (a Nuer Commander) declared defection to Machar. The Nuer White Army also quickly mobilized and sent reinforcement to Division 8 in Bor to mount a counter-offensive on Juba. In Juba, Dinkas resorted to tracking down Nuers in the City, indiscriminately killing them in their thousands. In the towns of Bor, Bentiu, Akobo and Malakal captured by Machar forces, Nuer fighters slaughtered Dinka civilians in revenge. When the government forces (predominantly Dinka) recaptured Bor, Dinka youth attacked the United Nations Mission in South Sudan (UNIMIS) compound and slaughtered some of Nuer civilians taking refuge in the compound. At that point, Nuers in government-controlled areas were not safe anymore, and the same with Dinkas in Nuer held territory. Source: *Agany, T 2014*

References

Agany, T. (2013, '). 'understanding the tribal, political and economic aspects of the current south Sudan civil war and their complications in achieving a peaceful, lasting solution. Sudantribune.

Biar, M. Z. (2013,). Z *Tribalism in South Sudan,*. www.sudantribune/spip.php?article51002.

Bryce, H. (2013). *the Dangers of Tribalism in South Sudan.* https://www.chathamhouse.org/media/comment/view/196439.

Deng, F. M. (2010). *Self-Determination and national unity, a challenge for Africa.* Asmara,: Saverance Publishing services.

Hirlinger, H. (2013). *What is 'tribalism' and why does it matter in South Sudan.* http://www.academia.edu/5517121/What_is_tribalism_and_why_does_it_matter_in_South_Sudan.

Turabi, H. (2013). *Interview on the wake of 2013 south Sudanese conflict.*

(n.d.). Youth against Tribalism in African. http://yatia.cfsites.org/custom.php?pageid=37000.

Understanding the Tribal... http://allafrica.com/stories/201412310553.html

Chapter Five
Religious contribution to ethnic conflicts

"Religion is defined as a philosophy of discipline concerned with the philosophical appraisal of human religious attitudes and of the real or imaginary objects of those attitudes, God or the gods (Encyclopedia Britannica)."

The role that religious communities continue to play in the modern world politics and general communal life is understood and interpreted differently. On one hand, there is a belief that in effect, religion contributes tremendously to the harmonization of the world. This understanding is aided by the assumption that most of the world religions teach peace, love, reconciliation and tranquility. For example, the two world major religions (Christianity and Islam) used the words peace, love, reconciliation, unity more than any other texts ever written on the planet earth.

It is thus assumed in this context that religion is something that people cannot comfortably live without it implications being embraced. Arguably, to continuously enjoy peaceful living, sharing of the wealth equitably and transparently is religiously paramount. Religious ethos must be practiced in later and spirit so that the world is made peaceful, joyous and conducive for all creatures inhabiting the earth.

On the contrary, since the days immortal, religion has contributed enormously to most of the obnoxious conflicts, taking place in the world. Although fingers are pointed to fanatics of religions, it is worthwhile to note that many followers of the world religions do not live their professed ethos, and this has precipitated occurrences of wars. Etymologically, religious conflicts started in what many religious followers believed as heaven.

The Scriptures in the Bible and Koran are clear about major rebellion against God by his once favoured angel. There are narrative and a well-known story about the Battle in Heaven: Lucifer, who was once God's favourite angel, is stated to have been prideful and decided to stage first ever, coup against heaven's ruler (God).

As part of his strategies, Lucifer formed a large group of angels under his command that then attacked the presidential guards angels unit who remained loyal to God; as expected in such situation, these loyal angels led by Michael the head of absolute angels battled. The fighting ensued, and the well-resourced God's angels prevailed and were victorious and Lucifer (Satan) and his disloyal Angels (Demons) were cast into Hell. Although, the author of the Bible had not captured in more details about the actual battle as it concentrates more on the solution than the problem.

Apparently there are verses scattered around that give us just enough perspectives to see that this fight indeed took place. The first scripture that comes to mind would have to be Revelation 12: 7-12, this story is well spelled out here below.

> **7 And there was war in heaven. Michael and his angels fought against the dragon, and the dragon and his angels fought back. 8 But he was not strong enough, and they lost their place in heaven. 9 The great dragon was hurled down; that ancient**

serpent called the devil, or Satan, who leads the whole world astray. He was thrown to the earth, and his angels with him (Rev 12: 7-12).

This story is widely believed as the true word of the scriptures written by people inspired by the Holy Spirit, backdated how old the notion of conflicts and implicated the religion in conflict is not only a contemporary issue. Before alluding to unpack the contemporary religious conflicts, I must first discuss religions followed by South Sudanese in particular.

Like any other citizens of the world, South Sudanese are followers of various faiths. The Pew Research Centre suggests that about 60% of the South Sudanese populations are Christian, with around 25% following Islam and 15% following African Traditional Religion (ATR) and animists. These figures may not be accurate as there has been no down to earth census. However, they provide a basis to make an argument such as in my writing here (see the below graphs).

Figure 4: Main Religious Groups in South Sudan

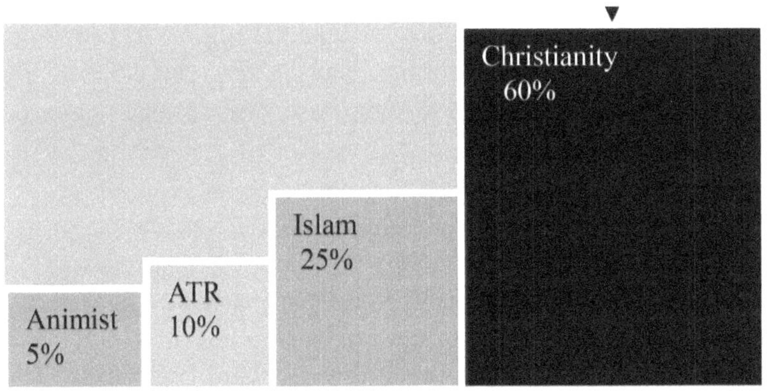

Christianity 60%
Islam 25%
ATR 10%
Animist 5%

Source: Author, Deng, J 2015

These main religious groups are subdivided into further groups, for example, in Christianity, there are numerous denominations. According to recently formed South Sudan Council of Churches (SSCC), there are eleven churches currently serving under the SSCC. These include: Africa Inland Church – Sudan, Catholic Church, Coptic Orthodox Church, Episcopal Church of the Sudan, Ethiopian Orthodox Church, Greek Catholic Church, Greek Orthodox Church (Patriarchate Alexandria), and Presbyterian Church of the Sudan, Sudan Evangelical Presbyterian Church, Sudan Interior Church, Sudan Pentecostal Church, and Sudanese Church of Christ. I grew up in the Episcopal Church of Sudan (a similar church with the Anglican), trained and ordained as a minister in 1999 after completing theological training. In this church, I have experienced what religious conflicts entailed.

The Province of the Episcopal of Sudan in recent years has been known for the occurrences of conflicts, divisions and leadership rivaling. Indeed, the administration rivaling in this church first reached the climax in the 1980s when two Archbishops competed over leadership of one province. One bishop, who was Archbishop at the time but canonically expected to retire, refused to withdraw. This refusal triggered anger and one other bishop who had eyed the archbishopric, declared and made himself Archbishop of Sudan subsequently consecrated four new bishops.

This drama nearly put the church apart, but the leadership of the Anglican Communion worldwide intervened and through it, all the consecrated bishops were confirmed. The Consecrated Bishops then included the present Archbishop Daniel Deng Bul of the Episcopal Church of South Sudan and Sudan. The divisions within the Church have continued especially in the mother Diocese of Bor where a significant number of senior clergymen defected to various denominations. Although the causes of these conflicts are rooted in a lack of proper education, training, poor church administration, lack of proper assignment of ordained ministers and finally the over- ordination of new individuals to the priesthood. Still today, in the Episcopal of the Sudan and South Sudan, there are many senior new priests serving in the Church.

Thus, most of the churches led by these priests, lack progress and conflicts, and divisions are daily occurrences. For example, In America, a certain priest came to Washington Dc as a refugee, and this priest was severely illiterate. He was received by a young priest who came years before him and had a congregation established. The senior priest demanded to take over the leadership of the church within a week of his arrival. He invited one elder to facilitate his carrying takingover of the Church that he rarely knew anybody but has a severe lack of knowledge of how administration works especially in a new enviroment.

Indeed, the young priest was innocent and had prepared the handling over at a later time when the new senior priest is settled and that he is familiar with the people, environment and the ministry as a whole. However when this demand was made repeately and intimidating to the educated young priest, the young priest decided to hand the church over to the new senior priest (newcomer). The members of the church were discouraged by the improper handling over of the leadership to the new senior priest who is severely illiterate and untrained. The Church, which was once united, became divided under the the socall senior priest. After a few years, the members of the congregation left to open their separate groups and hatred ensued between these congregations. This case study shows how most of the conflicts emerged in regious communities.

As read above; a significant number of conflicts in religious circles are ignited by poorly trained religious leaders. Such categories of religious leaders don't know how to govern let alone how to lead. Realistically, the sanctuaries are disgraced by such leaders. In this relation, Dyer a consultant on religious conflicts argues, "it seems illogical, Jesus called his disciples to love one another, and He gave them the Holy Spirit and was supposed to be on the path of transformation (Dyer 2015). Dyer pioneered a theory through his argument that some contributing factors continue to play significant roles in both internal and external religious conflicts.

In his view, the contributing factors to internal religious conflicts include the notion that, religious followers are a group of volunteers, extremely diverse, collectively seeking change and deeply held beliefs. He argues: "This potent combination, he says, is made worse by the fact Christians feel they should be the most peaceful community on earth, which creates an atmosphere of denial.

This tempted organizations not to acknowledge that conflict has taken place. And so very often it is forced underground by the fact that nobody wants to face the reality that we're struggling to get along together. So for that reason, the church in my experience is highly prone to conflict.

Figure 5: Factors contributing to internal religious conflicts

(http://www.biblesociety.org.au/news/conflict-church#sthash.u8VaT3pk.dpuf).

On the other hand, some other religious followers don't immerse in hatred and conflicts even if they are severely affected by the religious conflict. For example, Lana Obradovic, a student from Bosnia-Herzegovina who lost many relatives in the religious conflict there during the 1990s said this "the war changed everything in my life, and I was one of the thousands forced to leave during the ethnic cleansing in my city. But they did not manage to break me. I have NOT learned to hate my neighbours and I never will. (Obradovic 1990)". Similarly, Dr. Mahathir Mohamad, the Prime Minister of Malaysia, in his address during the World Evangelical Fellowship (on 2001-MAY-4. 4) said this:

> "Intolerance breeds injustice. Injustice invariably leads to rebellion and retaliation, and these will result in escalation on the part of both making reconciliation almost impossible. It would appear that during times of stress, despair and frustration, people become increasingly irrational, and they do things that they never think they are capable of doing. And so we see appalling brutality perpetrated by the gentlest people. "Once started, religious strife has a tendency to go on and on, to become permanent feuds. Today we see such intractable inter-religious wars in Northern Ireland, between Jews and Muslims and Christians in Palestine, Hindus and Muslims in South Asia and many other places. Attempts to

bring about peace have failed again and again. Always the extremist elements invoking past injustices, imagined or real, will succeed in torpedoing the peace efforts and bringing about another bout of hostility (Mohamed 2001)."

The role of religion in civil unrest and wars

Often, the media does not identify the precise causes of some of the conflicts around the world. Clashes are frequently described as being ethnic in origin, even though religion may have been the primary reason. The actual causes of unrest are sometimes difficult to determine. Frequently, there are a mixture of political alliances, economic differences, ethnic feuds, religious differences, and others: In Northern Ireland, "the troubles" refer to about three decades of violence, largely between the Roman Catholics nationalist community who sought union with Ireland and the primarily Protestant unionist community who want to remain part of the UK. It was mostly rooted in discrimination by the Protestant majority against the Catholic minority. Between 1969 and 2001, 3,526 people were killed by Republican and Loyalist paramilitary groups and by British and Irish security forces. An uneasy peace was attained by the Belfast Agreement of 1998 and has endured.

The Rwanda genocide was mainly an ethnic conflict between the Hutu majority and the Tutsi minority. The religious split in the country (75% Christian, mostly Roman Catholic, and 25% indigenous) appears not to have been a significant factor. On the order of 800,000 Tutsi and moderate Hutu were murdered, between 1994-APR to July, mostly by being hacked to death. The war in Bosnia-Herzegovina was among three faith groups, (Muslim, Roman Catholic, and Serbian Orthodox). The Serbian Orthodox Christian attacks on Muslims are sufficiently severe to rise to the level of genocide.

The horrendous civil war in Sudan, called the Second Sudanese Civil War, lasted from 1983 to 2005; it had a significant religious component among Muslims, Christians and Animists. But inter-tribal warfare, racial and language conflicts are also involved. About two million died directly or indirectly during the war (Sectarian unrest). The conflict has eased. A peace agreement of 2005 led to a referendum and independence for southern Sudan, which is known as the Republic of South Sudan.

The Second Congo War (a.k.a. Africa's World War and the Great War of Africa) started in 1998 in the Democratic Republic of the Congo. By 2008, 5.4 million people had been killed, largely by disease and starvation. Hostilities continue to the present. A group of world religious leaders from the Buddhist, Protestant, Catholic and Orthodox Christian, Jewish, Muslim and many other faiths met in Geneva Switzerland during 1999-OCT. They issued a document, The Geneva Spiritual Appeal, asking political and religious leaders and organizations to ensure that religions are not used to justify violence in the future.

Delegates believed that many of the then current 56 conflicts have religious elements. It is important to realize that most of the world's current "hot spots" have a complex interaction of economic, racial, ethnic, religious, and other factors. I listed below some of the conflicts that have religious connotations as precipitator.

Figure 6: contemporary religious inclined conflicts

Nation	Religious groups	Brief conflict narrative
Afghanistan	Extreme, radical Fundamentalist Muslim terrorist groups & non-Muslims	• Osama bin Laden headed a terrorist group called Al Quada. They were protected by, and integrated with, the Taliban dictatorship in the country. The Northern Alliance of rebel Afghans, Britain and the U.S. attacked the Taliban and Al Quada, establishing a new regime in part of the country. The fighting continues
Bosnia	Serbian Orthodox Christians, Roman Catholic), Muslims	• Fragile peace is holding, due to the presence of peacekeepers.

Côte d'Ivoire	Côte d'Ivoire Muslims, Indigenous, Christian	• Following the elections in late 2000, government security forces began targeting civilians solely and explicitly on the basis of their religion, ethnic group, or national origin. • The overwhelming majority of victims come from the largely Muslim north of the country, or are immigrants or the descendants of immigrants...A military uprising continued the slaughter in 2002. • It split the nation into two segments. Periods of peace and violence have alternated as the country struggles towards stability.
Cyprus	Christians & Muslims	• The island is partitioned, creating enclaves for ethnic Greeks (Christians) and Turks (Muslims) and UN peace keeping force is maintaining stability.

East Timor	Christians & Muslims	• About 30% of the population died by murder, starvation or disease after they were forcibly annexed by Indonesia (mainly Muslim). • After voting for independence, many Christians were exterminated or exiled by the Indonesian army and army-funded militias in a carefully planned program of genocide and religious cleansing.
India	Animists, Christians, Hindus, Muslims & Sikhs	• Various conflicts that heat up periodically producing loss of life. Christians are regularly attacked in Orissa province by militant Hindu extremists.
Indonesia, Maluku Islands	Christians & Muslims	• Conflicts between Christians and Muslims started during 1999. About 6,000 were killed; over a half million people were internally displaced; thousands were forced to convert to another religion. Peace talks were initiated by the government in early 2002. The situation appears to be more stable with sporadic outbreaks of violence.

Iraq	Kurds, Shiite Muslims, Sunni Muslims, Yazidi	• For decades, one group has controlled the government, and the other two groups have suffered. In 2014, a new group invaded the country: ISIS By mid-2006, a small scale civil war, primarily between Shiite and Sunni Muslims started.
Kashmir	Hindus & Muslims	• A chronically unstable region of the world, claimed by both Pakistan and India. Thirty to sixty thousand people have died since 1989.
Kosovo	Serbian Orthodox Christians & Muslims	• There is convincing evidence of past mass murder by Yugoslavian government (mainly Serbian Orthodox Christians) against ethnic Albanians (mostly Muslim)
Kurdistan	Christians, Muslims	• Periodic assaults on Christians (Protestant, Chaldean Catholic, & Assyrian Orthodox).
Macedonia	Macedonian Orthodox Christians & Muslims	• Muslims (often referred to as ethnic Albanians) engaged in a civil war with the rest of the country who are primarily Macedonian Orthodox Christians during the 1990s
Middle East	Jews, Muslims, & Christians	• Major strife broke out in 2000-SEP. Flare-ups repeat. No resolution appears possible.

Nigeria	Christians, Animists, & Muslims	• Yourubas and Christians in the south of the country are battling Muslims in the north. Country is struggling towards democracy after decades of Muslim military dictatorships. Recently Boko Aram abducted girls
Northern Ireland	Protestants, Catholics	• 30 years over 3,600 people were killed and assassinated.
Pakistan	Sunni & Shi'ite Muslims	• Low level mutual attacks, overshadowed by Taliban insurrectionists
Philippines	Christians & Muslims	• A low level conflict between the mainly Christian central government and Muslims in the south of the country has continued for centuries
Russia, Chechnya	Russian Orthodox Christians, Muslims	• In January 2002 Chechen rebels included all Christians on their list of official enemies, vowing to 'blow up every church and mission-related facility in Russia'." 7
Somalia	Wahhabi and Sufi Muslims	• Sufi Muslims -- a tolerant moderate tradition of Islam are fighting the Shabab who follow the Wahhabi tradition of Islam in a continuing conflict.
South Africa	Animists & "Witches"	• Hundreds of persons, suspected and accused of witches practicing black magic, are murdered each year.

South Sudan	Christians	• Cush International Church destroyed, & church personnel arrested
Sri Lanka	Buddhists & Hindus	• Tamils (a mainly Hindu 18% minority) are involved in a war aimed at dividing the island and creating a homeland for themselves. • Conflict had been underway since 1983 with the Sinhalese Buddhist majority (70%). Over a hundred thousand people have been killed. The conflict took a sudden change for the better in 2002-SEP, when the Tamils dropped their demand for complete independence. By 2009 the Tamil uprising was crushed by the government
Sudan	Animists, Christians & Muslims	• Complex ethnic, racial, religious conflict in which the Muslim regime committed genocide against both Animists and Christians in the south of the country. Slavery and near slavery were practiced. A ceasefire was signed in 2006-MAY between some of the combatants. 3 Warfare continues in the Darfur region, primarily between a Muslim militia and Muslim inhabitants

Thailand	Buddhists & Muslims	• Muslim rebels have been involved in a bloody insurgency in southern Thailand -- a country that is 95% Buddhist
Tibet	Buddhists & Communists	• Country was annexed by Chinese Communists in late 1950's. Brutal suppression of Buddhism continues
Uganda	Animists, Christians, & Muslims	• Christian rebels of the Lord's Resistance Army are conducting a civil war in the north of Uganda. Their goal is a Christian theocracy whose laws are based on the Ten Commandments. They abduct, enslave and/or raped about

Source: //www.religioustolerance.org/curr_war.htm

As read from the above cases scenarios, a majority of the past and present, world conflicts, originated from a religious feuds and conflicts. Although, I believed that religions still and can play significant roles in bringing about world peace. This could however in effect only happen if the religious communities have restored its lost ethical and moral teaching, which is achievable by engaging in the thorough training of religious spokespersons and those in charge of religious institutions. The importance of training workers in any field such as in the religious circles is well emphasized in the Management study guide. It is argued that "training is crucial for organizational development and success. It is fruitful to both employers and employees of an organization. An employee in any institution will become more efficient and productive if they are trained well in the skill required in the job.
(www.managementstudyguide.com/training-of-employees.htm)."

Also, there is a common saying in South Sudan that "little education is sickness and without education, it is like being dead (Anonymous)." It is also said that an empty tin makes noise. This is true with the religious leaders with little education or with no primary education. Such leaders remain vulnerable to forms or create a cult, promote heresies also known as wrong teachings. For example, the majority of Islamic extremists and fighters around the world are believed to be those from the little economic background, especially high school drops out and those with lives full of complexities regarding quick family breakdown and engagement in drugs.

References

D, T. (2015). Conflict in the church. /www.biblesociety.org.au/news/conflict-church#sthash.u8VaT3pk.dpuf

Forsberg, M. I. (1964). *Dry season : today's church crisis in the Sudan; the development of the church in the Sudan, East Africa and the events leading to the expulsion of missionaries* . New York: Sudan Interior Mission.

Hardy, C. (2013). *History of christianity* . http://prezi.com/ows2ltegawpl/christianity/.

Kung, H. (n.d.). *Peace-Tripod.* http://lumpykarma.tripod.com/images/peace.html

(n.d.). little education is sickness.

(n.d.). *management guide.* www.managementstudyguide.com/training-of-employees.htm).

(n.d.). *Prayer and l war.* http://kuyah.blogspot.com/2009/01/prayer-war.html

(n.d.). *Religiously based civil unrest and warfare.* http://www.religioustolerance.org/curr_war.htm.

(n.d.). *Why do you believe in god?* http://www.shroomery.org/forums/showflat.php/Number/10629734

Mahathir, M. P. (2001). Malaysian Prime Minister) address during the World Evangelical Fellowship.

Chapter Six
South Sudan as failed and fragile State

The state had the obligation to ensure equal opportunities to all its citizens, elimination of exploitation and discrimination, and to provide needed social services such as education, medical care and social security. It was expected therefore that members of the State would contribute willingly and without stint, to the development of the nation (Waanglicana, 2013).

The Republic of South Sudan in the survey conducted by the Fragile State Index (FSI) in 2014 was found among the few failed states in the modern world. The Fragile States Index survey is conducted yearly and squarely among 178 nations based on their levels of stability and the pressures that face them in governance, and in the national building.

This initiative is funded by the Global Funds for Peace (FP), an Independent, nonpartisan organization that continues to conduct surveys on fragile states globally. However, the study is set on the criteria formulated by FSI, which defined fail states as countries that are inundated by the rampant existence of arms conflicts, weak institutions, poor governance, political instability, corruptions and lack of societal cohesion as a result. Here below are twelve social and economic indicators that FSI used to measure success and fallibility as a state.

Figure 7: Twelve Social and Economic Indicators

1. Demographic Pressures	2. Refugees and IDPs	3. Uneven Economic Development
• Natural Disasters • Disease • Environment • Pollution • Water Scarcity • Population Growth • Youth Bulge • Mortality • Food Scarcity • Malnutrition	• Displacement • Refugee Camps • IDP Camps • Disease related to Displacement • Refugees per capita • IDPs per capita • Absorption capacity	• GINI Coefficient • Income Share of highest 10% • Income Share of lowest 10% • Urban-Rural Service Distribution • Access to Improved Services • Slum Population
4. Group Grievance	**5. Human Flight and Brain Drain**	**6. Poverty and Economic Decline**
• Discrimination • Powerlessness • Ethnic Violence • Communal Violence • Sectarian Violence • Religious Violence	• Migration per capita • Human Capital • Emigration of Educated Population	• Economic Deficit • Government Debt • Unemployment • Youth Employment • Purchasing Power • GDP per capita • GDP Growth • Inflation

7. State Legitimacy	8. Public Services	9. Human Rights and Rule of Law
• Corruption • Government • Effectiveness • Political • Participation • Electoral Process • Level of Democracy • Illicit Economy • Drug Trade • Protests and • Demonstrations • Power Struggles	• Policing • Criminality • Education Provision • Literacy • Water & Sanitation • Infrastructure • Quality Healthcare • Telephony • Internet Access • Energy Reliability • Roads	• Press Freedom • Civil Liberties • Political Freedoms • Human Trafficking • Political Prisoners • Incarceration • Religious • Persecution • Torture • Executions
10. Security Apparatus	11. Factionalized Elites	12. External Intervention
• Internal Conflict • Small Arms • Proliferation • Riots and Protests • Fatalities from • Conflict • Military Coups • Rebel Activity • Militancy • Bombings • Political Prisoners	• Power Struggles • Defectors • Flawed Elections • Political • Competition	• Foreign Assistance • Presence of Peace keepers • Presence of UN • Missions • Foreign Military • Intervention • Sanctions • Credit Rating

Source: http://library.fundforpeace.org/fsi14-overviewf

Many South Sudanese argue against the fail state narrative, they instead, believe that South Sudan was born from a scratch, and thus has no infrastructure, no capacity for governance and that the nation only has the army that emerged from rebel movements. Arguably South Sudan inheritance from the old Sudan, amount to an absolute nothing. Dr. Garang in one of his discourses affirmed this in his statement, and I quote "there has been no road since the time of creation in South Sudan." Indeed, this report depicted and confirmed a present reality of South Sudan's primitively.

In this context, South Sudanese project the fallibility of the country to the old Sudan, blaming it entirely on the successive governments in Khartoum. South Sudan in their view, is not a failed state but a new state facing challenges of governance. Hence, they refute the labeling of South Sudan as a fail state. Although, there are elements of truths in the argument presented, I personally on the opposite believe that South Sudan is a fail state. I also think that the arguments against a fail state narrative from South Sudan elites as paraded above, fall short of what I would call international standards and fall short on the criteria and framework used to measure the notion of a fail state.

It is expected that a functional state provides adequate and efficient services for its citizens. On the contrary, South Sudan is inundated by many humanitarian organizations trying to bridge the wide gap in the service delivery to the civil population in the country. To make matters worse, these relief and humanitarian organizations find it hard to access the affected and suffering masses of Sudan people accross the country.

The government, in about ten years between 2005- 2013, has received billions of US dollars from oil sales, and from non-oil revenues including customs tax. But this wealth, instead of bringing about development and intensifying service delivery to the South Sudanese, who have suffered for the last 50 years fighting to gain their independence, has ended up in coffers and in individual's accounts in foreign countries. The vice (corruption) that had never existed in the culture of South Sudanese people has destroyed and betrayed the hard fought and gained freedom.

We are a failed state whether we refuse it as this is the argument held by some South Sudanese. Understandably, it is the hard truth to take home that we are a fail state, and as we may try to shift responsibilities of such failure to one another or finger point others, our country tops the world failed states. The persisting question should not be how we failed as a country but rather how we should come out of the box of a failed state. According to the World Bank Institute (WBI), the following points help a failed state to reconstitute itself and become successful riding difficulties it once faces. These points include:

- ✓ Enhancing the capacity of the state at all levels - as well as civil society organizations, media and the private sector - to build, lead, and sustain coalitions for state-building, successful transitions, reform, and improved transparency and accountability.
- ✓ Capacity development and skills-building, with emphasis on revenue collection, budget management, procurement, service delivery, and associated monitoring and evaluation.
- ✓ Building in-country leadership skills to achieve results through implementation support to governmental and non-governmental teams.
- ✓ Mobilizing innovative technologies, including ICTs and the Global Development Learning Network (GDLN), to help governments and civil society to share knowledge and promote good governance. For example, an Innovation Fair - Moving beyond Conflict, in Cape Town in April

2010 - convened development practitioners, researchers, donors, and private sector firms to exchange innovations on conflict prevention and resolution, including ICT applications for improved governance and service delivery, tailored to situations of fragility and conflict.
- ✓ Supporting public private partnerships toward enhanced service delivery.
- ✓ Promoting improved governance and transparency in extractive industries (https://wbi.worldbank.org/wbi/about/topics/fragile-states).

In the lieu of the above points, South Sudan has an opportunity to resurrect from its current position to a better position. This potentiality exists in the context of reforms and an overhaul of the present evil governing the system. I am optimistic that South Sudan could in a very short time change its current status at the world stage if she adopts and implements the above six points. I, thus, concur with the six tick-points offered by the World Bank Institute (WBI). There is a need to embark on capacity development at both the state and central level of government. Ugaz, chair of Transparency International once urged "countries at the bottom need to adopt radical anti-corruption measures for their people (Ugaz 2014)." It is thus possible to produce effective professional public servants; people who would abide by the public services Acts and regulations, equipped to perform their duties and responsibilities diligently.

Unlike the present workforce full with incompetent workers brought in to work by their relatives and uncles just to earn money, but perform nothing, the labour force under a new paradigm, will be those well-trained individuals South Sudanese, somewhat selected on merits and appropriately placed on their deserving positions.

Secondly, there is the need to have active civil society organizations that hold values of fairness, working for efficient service delivery and advocate for the voice of the voiceless in the community. I am convinced that there are no credible civil society organizations in South Sudan as I write. All we have at the moment in the country, are government engineered agents, decorated in the name of civil society organizations but only serve to promote government agendas, they are in the contemporary term, referred to as briefcase organizations. In my view, I, propose that credible civil society organizations should emerge from its present tatters and build its capacity only to focus on people's needs; lobbying for their well-being through state authorities and other corporation.

Another important area of concern in national building is the establishment of independent media. In his article, the role of media in today's world, Muzna argues, "in the world of today, media has become as necessary as food and clothing. It has played a significant role in strengthening the society. Media is considered as "mirror" of the modern society, in fact, it is the media which shapes our lives (Muzna 2015)." South Sudan lacks the existence of independent media.

Although there are numerous media houses in the country, most of these media fraternities are excessively state controlled and as a result, have lost their media-independence. They have just become state propaganda machines. Muzna concludes, "If the media identifies its responsibility and work sincerely and honestly, then it can serve as significant force in building the nation (Muzna 2015)." This is achievable only if South Sudan enacts media laws that are not biased but laws that protect media houses and regulate their activities in a fair and lawful environment.

Above all, what is required in South Sudan is a change from a present status quo of a failed state to a producing state. In this relation, Lewin's changed model is worth exploring to understand a possible context of change in South Sudan. In his changed model, Lewin offers an understanding that the:

> "Level of behavior at any moment in time is the result of two set of forces: those striving to maintain the status quo and those pushing for change. When both sets of forces are equal, current levels of behavior are maintained in what Lewin termed a state of quasi-stationery equilibrium. To change that state, one can increase those forces pushing for change, decrease those forces that maintain the current state or apply some combination of both. (Waddel et al. 2014, p 33)."

In Lewin's view, making an effort to adjust forces that resist change to reduce tension is paramount. He in effect regarded change process as including three key steps: unfreezing, moving and refreezing. In the first step of unfreezing, the organization is giving options to choose from in terms of adopting one favourite, for example, showing a projection of a desired behaviour and actions at the current status quo.

Members are then exposed to make choices in the two situations. In the second step of the change process, the behaviours of the organization from the old situation to a new situation and develop new values and procedures. The third step to change process is what is called refreezing. This step establishes the organization at a new state of equilibrium. It requires reinforcement and support mechanism to provide comfort in a new state of being for the organization. Here below is the figure depicting the Lewin's planned model of change.

Figure 8: Lewin planned change model

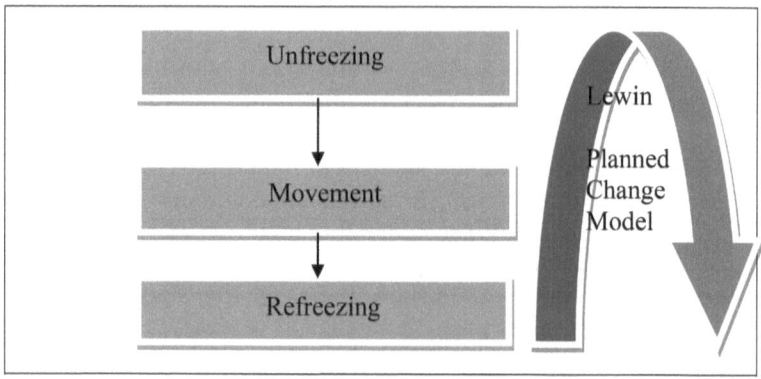

Source: Waddell et al. 2014, p35

The Lewin's model for change has some relevance to the prevailing situation in South Sudan. Before December 2013, there were voices calling for internal reforms within the governing structure as to adjust to failures that were seen encroaching into the country especially, corruption, insecurity, and political stability. These voices of change were resisted and squeezed to zip up while the nation was left bleeding. It did not take long before the country becomes a failed state.

In recent debates, South Sudan needs change although the forces resisting change are still high. There is a need to increase and advance forces pushing for change in South Sudan. This could be done in the context of stopping the war, reintroducing good governance and rirducing corruption in the country. As both forces offer extreme parallels positions, a combination of the bit of each side is worth consolidating. The proceeding chapter addresses institutional reforms as a pretext for bringing about changes and installation of good governance in the world newest country.

References

Index, F. S. (n.d.). http://library.fundforpeace.org/fsi14-overview.

Garang, J. (2005,). interview, no road in South Sudan since creation time".

Muzna, S. (2015). The role of media in today's world. http://www.hamariweb.com/articles/article.aspx?id=10166.

Waddell, D. C. (2014). , *Organizational change: Development and transformation.* Cengage Learning Australia Pty Limited.

Institute, w. B. (2014). *Fragile states.* https://wbi.worldbank.org/wbi/about/topics/fragile-states.

Ugaz, J. (2014,). *Corruption is threatening economic growth for all.* Transparency International,. http://www.transparency.org/cpi2014/results

Waanglicana. (2013). https://waanglicana.wordpress.com/2013/05/14/a-war-we-cannot-afford-to-loose-tribalism-in-kenya.

Chapter Seven
Institutional Reforms and Good Governance

"When government fears people, there is liberty. When people fear the government, there is tyranny" says by Thomas Jefferson, the former president of the US.

The louder cry by the people of South Sudan, their friends and well-wishers is solely about the existence pervasive bad governance and the lack of the rule of law in the nation. The world's youngest country has suffered much retrogressively due to the lack of the ingredients mentioned above. The South Sudanese ordinary men on the street continue to lament on the phrase 'If John Garang were here'... roads in the country would have been built, hospitals would have existed in quality and quantity, insecurity would have been a thing of the past, the vice, corruption would not have existed let alone being rampant, the borders of the country would have been cemented with perpetual peace and positive bilateral relations.

South Sudanese lamented that if John Garang were indeed here, South Sudan would be a bread basket of Africa. As an economist himself, John Garang would have invested heavily in agriculture and oil plus other natural resources in the country. But this is not the case, the rhetoric 'if John Garang was here', has become an agonizing phrase for many suffering

South Sudanese. However, the current ruling elites don't entertain the words of if John Garang was here; they instead believe that it is their time to rule and articulate policies in the country. Moses died before Israelites fully realized their freedom, but Joshua took over Moses and took people to the Promised Land. This is referenced to reflect the demise of John Garang (as Moses) and the elevation of Salva Kiir (Joshua) who became the first president of the Independent Republic of South Sudan. John Garang himself has predicted this current situation in one of the public lectures, and I quote:

> "Our blood will be shed because I hate oppression and marginalization of our people but I will not even enjoy the fruits of this struggle. There are people sleeping comfortably right now, they don't know the hunger or the sound of a gun. After our job is done that generation will take over; they will cut a large piece of land with pangas and sell it cheaply for a bottle of beer (Dr. John Garang De Mabior, speech 1992)."

Prophetically, this statement has relevance in South Sudan as I write this piece. There are a bunch of people especially those who were enjoying their lives in foreign countries, now holding strategic positions of influence in South Sudan. They are selling and grabbing land as they wish. They don't reflect on the years of the past because they were not there, and they completely lack the experience of the suffering of our people. The Hon Chol Tong Mayai (2013), once in his speech, referred to such people as foreigners ruling us in South Sudan. For they have no connection with the real life struggle of the masses of South Sudanese. Their children live in foreign countries enjoying luxurious life with money siphoned. They indeed cut a big chunk of land and sell it over a bottle of beer. Millions of land disappeared each day in the South capital cities only to be found registered under foreign names.

Good Governance

The question becomes what then do we need to do to rid off this chronic (bad governance) situation in the country? Of course, few options come to mind, one being the notion of reforms; others may call it overhaul of all public sectors in the country. Above all, South Sudan needs good governance to realign services to the people. According to the United Nations Economic and Social Commission (UNESCO), good management is defined as

> "...the process of decision-making and the process by which decisions are implemented effectively in public sector and good governance must be; participatory, consensus oriented, accountable, transparent, responsive, effective and efficient, equitable and inclusive and follows the rule of law. It assures that corruption is minimized, the views of minorities are taken into account and that the voices of the most vulnerable in society are heard in decision-making. It is also responsive to the present and future needs of society
>
> (http://www.unescap.org/sites/default/files/good-governance.pdf).

These eight characteristics of good governance should be embraced in South Sudan. Firstly, we need participatory governance where power is solely base with people, and that power is used for the benefit of people, for example, the security forces in the country should be only meant to protect people and their properties, and not to kill people and loot their properties. Secondly, all levels of government must act on consensus but not on the individual institution. For example, the prevailing situation in the country was caused by non-adherence to a consensus decision-making right from the presidency. Thus, the unconstitutional removal of state governors and the untimely dismissal of the first Vice President are few classical examples where consensus approach was ignored.

Thirdly, South Sudan is ranked in the first row of the world most corrupt countries (Transparent International, 2014). South Sudan has never fought any successful cases of corruption. The Country has a whole had never followed accountability, in this relation, Ken Scott, a research consultant for Amnesty International in South Sudan once said "and among the root causes of the South Sudan problems are an unfortunate culture of impunity and a historical absence of accountability (Scott 2014)." This absence of accountability measures has made this country to slip into the world worse failed and corrupt state. As an ingredient of good governance, accountability measures must always be taken to ensure that everyone is accountable for the mistake he or she has committed in the course of rendering services.

Fourthly, Transparency in public service is vital to national prosperity. It is believed that national unity is reflected in the way people get jobs in public service. In South Sudan, it is all about nepotism, people get jobs from their relatives that comprise the notion of meritocracy and competent based employment. If South Sudan is to be known as a country observing transparency, it must start from the basic such as the work of public service employees. There must be radical changes in human resources management policies in the country so as to give rooms to fairness and transparency.

Fifthly, effective and efficient are essential ingredients of good governance. Efficiency in the context of good governance also covers the sustainable use of natural resources and the protection of the environment. Dr. Garang once said that his government would use the oil money to diversify the national economy. He had in mind the concept of efficiency, using what is available to inject other sectors to produce wealth in abundance and create prosperity in the nation. This concept has been utilized in the western world where one sector of the economy is used to stimulate the other.

Sixth, equitable and inclusive approach to good governance is crucial in the service delivery. According to the United Nations Economic and Social Commission:

> "A society's wellbeing depends on ensuring that all its members feel that they have a stake in it and do not feel excluded from the mainstream of society. This requires all groups, but particularly the most vulnerable, have opportunities to improve or maintain their well-being." Source…
> (http://www.unescap.org/sites/default/files/good-governance.pdf)."

South Sudan is a polarized society as a result of the recent conflict that has engulfed the whole country. People talk of tribes; there is emphasis on regional politics at all levels of government. South Sudanese seems to have forgotten their South Sudanese-ness and embark on their tribes as the focal point. We have in this relations, seen the formation of an ethnic council such Jieeng Council, Council of equatorian and Nuer councils respectively. This is what I would call the ethnicization of South Sudan politics on which this book aims to eradicate. All these are a result of bad governance, resorted into ethnic identities.

Seventh, the responsive government has much to do with how it coordinates services and policies in a way that embraces the input of stakeholders. In Australia, government policies are formulated through ideas, needs and priorities of the public through the work of lobbyists and think tanks. Most of the systems in Australia culminate from evidence-based. On the contrary, South Sudan lacks the existence of lobbyists and well-equipped think-tanks that could help policy makers produce people-based policies. The ministers in South Sudan instead make policies on their discretions that in most cases have been the recipe of failures and under development.

Eight, the existence of the useful rule of laws and their implementation in a given country, defined a nature of a state. This particular characteristic of good governance is paramount; the rule of law requires that a full protection of human rights is given, particularly to those of minorities. Secondly, there has to be impartial enforcement of legislation without favoritism or twisting.

In an ideal world, nobody is to be above the law, even Heads of States or call them Prime Ministers respectively. In South Sudan, laws are not being understood, or they are not impartially implemented. The picture below shows how members of civil society have started campaigning against corruption in South Sudan.

We have seen cases, where the laws are tuned to favor individuals, for example, South Sudan transitional constitution was made just to target institutions and persons to exercise control. In effect, the laws gave individuals and institutions excessive powers such as in the case of national security laws at the expense of individuals and innocent civilians. If fair laws are introduced.

In many first world countries, the laws are made above men and women of all calibers and status in the societies. The laws when broken, pull down people to face the full force of the law irrespective of their positions and status.

In Queensland State Government in Australia, a Minister for Labor Mr. Gordon Nuttal was jailed for seven years after he was found guilty of misappropriating funds and receiving $150,000 in a kickback with a business person Mr. Brendan McKennariey

(http://www.theguardian.com/australia-news/2015/jul/20/former-queensland-labor-minister-gordon-nuttall-released-from-jail).

Contextually, Mr. Gordon Nuttall's story fitted well with the story of Mr. Arthur Akuien, former South Sudan Minister of Finance who was accused of embezzling millions of dollars from the treasury during his tender as a minister. Unlike the case of Gordon Nuttall, Arthur Akuien stills to this day a free man enjoying grabbed riches.

The Dura saga worth of millions of dollars disappeared between State Governors and non-governmental organizations contracted. Still today, nobody has faced the full force of the law. The $ 4 billion have been siphoned and nobody has been charged. The so call 75 letters of the president of the Republic of South Sudan, to former and current ministers asking them to return money stolen was a failed strategy.

Truthfully, nothing tangible beyond the 75 letters written was heard and, money has gone into the pockets of individuals in both government and private. However, despite this obnoxious practice, I have no doubt in my mind that South Sudan could be a better country if she adopts to observe laws as part of the quest for good governance.

Figure 9: Characteristics of good governance

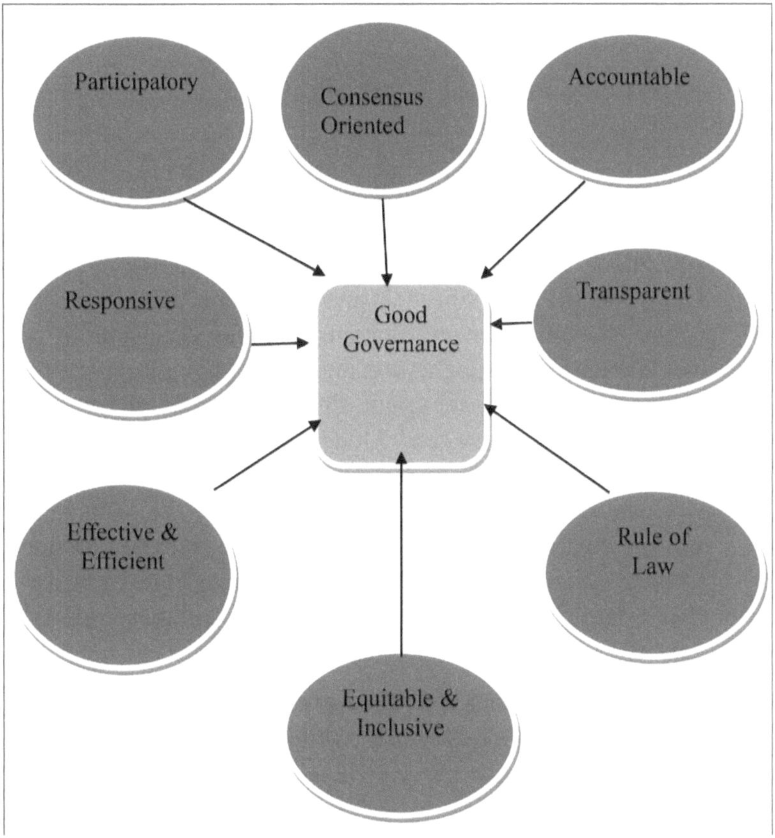

```
   Participatory    Consensus        Accountable
                    Oriented

   Responsive  →   Good Governance  ←  Transparent

   Effective &                          Rule of
   Efficient                            Law

                   Equitable &
                   Inclusive
```

(http://www.unescap.org/sites/default/files/good-governance.pdf)

Similarly Anderson (1989, 19-22), outlined seven key roles of a functioning government. In his view, these functions include the provision of economic infrastructure, provision of various collective goods and services, resolution and adjustment of group conflicts, maintenance of competition, protection of national resources, providing minimum access for individuals to the products and services of the economy and stabilization of the economy. In the ideal world, these are universal functions of a government. Anderson has highlighted these features in the box below.

Functions of government as explained by Anderson (1989, pp19-22):

- Providing economic infrastructure: Governments provide the basic institutions, rules and arrangements necessary for the satisfactorily operation of a modern capitalist system. These include the definition and protection of a property rights, the enforcement of contracts, the provision of a standard currency, weights and measures, corporate charters, bankruptcy, patents, copyright, the maintenance of law and order and the tariff system. Modern economic societies are political ones as well; it would be not be possible for the economic system to operate without rules of the game and the framework for the economic life being provided by the political system. Contracts are legally binding because of the laws established by the state and backed, in last resort, by state sanctions.

- Provision of various collective goods and services: There are some public goods which, while valuable to the whole society, are difficult for individuals to pay for according to the amount of good used. Once provided for one, they are available for all. These include such items as national defence, roads and bridges, aids to navigation, flood control, sewage disposal, traffic control system, and other infrastructure. Many are characterized by their broad use, indivisibility and non-excludability and are, therefore, public goods.

- The resolution and adjustment of group's conflicts: A basic reason for the existence of government is the need to resolve or ameliorate conflict in a society in pursuance of justice, order and stability. This may include actions to protect the economically weak against the economically strong. Government may seek to replace exploitation with equity through child labor laws, minimum wage legislation, or workers compensation programmes.

- The maintenance of competition: Competition does not always maintain itself in the private sector and government action is often required to ensure that businesses to do compete. Without government monitoring, the benefits of the free enterprise system would not necessarily appear. In absence of suitable regulation, companies would be able to form cartels, restrict access to their products and fix prices.

- Protection of natural resources: Competitive forces cannot be relied on to prevent the wasteful use of natural resources, to protect against degradation of the natural environment, or to care for the interests of future generations. Damage to the environment from market activity is the textbook example of externality and market failure. Only government can alleviate environmental damage.

- Minimum access by individuals to the goods and services of the economy: The operation of the market sometimes produces results that are cruel or socially unacceptable-poverty, unemployment, malnutrition-in their impact on people. Others because of illness, old age, literacy, or whatever, may simply exist outside the market economy. There is often disagreement over level of assistance, the aggregate cost and particular programmes which may have some social costs.

- Stabilization of the economy: There have been fluctuations in the business cycle of the economy where boom conditions are followed by recessions. Government action may be able to alleviate these through the budget, or monetary policy or control over wages or prices. Although government action is often imperfect and sometimes wrong, the community regards the government as being responsible for the state of the economy and there is a public expectation that governments should act to try to solve any problem (Anderson 1989, pp 19-22).

The seven roles of government explored by Anderson are in effect, universal; they are the genre functions of any governments anywhere in the world. To bring this to the perspective of a failed state, one could readily understand that failed states are those countries and nations with limited capacity or are rigid to function entirely on the above roles. South Sudan is a good example of a government that fails to execute some of its basic functions.

Firstly, the economy infrastructure of a country has collapsed, affected by the recent 2013 conflict. Secondly, the government has no services to deliver to the society that is in desperate need of such goods and services.

Thirdly, it has failed to adjust or solve group's conflicts including issues facing the country. The Honorable Onyoti, a minority leader representing SPLM-DC in the South Sudan Legislative Assembly (SSLA), summarized the prevailing national problems as including cattle raiding, bad governance, indiscipline security forces, breeding tribalism and 2013 Riek-Kiir conflicts. He asserted that the government of Juba especially the SPLM ruling party is incapable of solving not even one single of these problems, let alone all of these problems mentioned (Onyoti, SSTV interview by Face the Nation program, 2015).

Fourthly, there is non-existence of competition laws; instead the little market is monopolized by few individuals, and heavily resourced by corrupt officials to do their shady deals at the expense of fairness and equity to all citizens. A good example of this was the so call letters of credits (LC). After seeing a scarcity of hard currency in the market caused by insecurity in the country, the government decided to give out Letters of Credits to revive the market; reintroduce hard currency to facilitate import of goods and services to the country. Contrary to this goal, the letters of credits got into wrong hands that used them as a commodity instead, selling them through rocking black market prices.

Fifthly, natural resources are not adequately protected; there are rumors that illegal poachers killed animals daily, for instant one Chinese man was caught at the Juba International Airport, boarding with bags full of elephants horns, there is rampant illegal gold mining in East Equatoria State (ES) especially in Kapoeta County area. These practices existed due to lack of adequate natural resources protection mechanism.

Sixth, there is massive unemployment with no tangible initiative in place to alleviate massive unemployment in the country. Seventh, the economy is not stable and is severely fragile. According to South Sudan Economy 2015 by CIA World Factbook, the economy of South Sudan is summarized as follows:

> Following several decades of civil war with Sudan, industry and infrastructure in landlocked South Sudan are severely underdeveloped and poverty is widespread. Subsistence agriculture provides a living for the vast majority of the population. Property rights are insecure and price signals are weak, because markets are not well organized. South Sudan has little infrastructure - approximately 250 of paved roads. Electricity is produced mostly by costly diesel generators and indoor plumbing and potable water are scarce. South Sudan depends largely on imports of goods, services, and capital - mainly from Uganda, Kenya and Sudan. Nevertheless, South Sudan does have abundant natural resources. At independence in 2011, South Sudan produced nearly three-fourths of former Sudan's total oil output of nearly a half million barrels per day. The government of South Sudan derives nearly 98% of its budget revenues from oil. Oil is exported through two pipelines that run to refineries and shipping facilities at Port Sudan on the Red Sea. The economy of South Sudan will remain linked to Sudan for some time, given the

long lead time and great expense required to build another pipeline, should the government decide to do so. In January 2012 South Sudan suspended production of oil because of its dispute with Sudan over transhipment fees. This suspension lasted fifteen months and had a devastating impact on GDP, which declined by 48% in 2012. With the resumption of oil flows the economy rebounded strongly during the second half of calendar year 2013. This occurred in spite of the fact that oil production, at an average level of 222,000 barrels per day, was 40% lower compared with 2011, prior to the shutdown. GDP is estimated to have grown by about 25% in 2013. However, the outbreak of conflict on December 15, 2013 combined with a further reduction of oil exports, means that GDP growth forecasts for 2014 are being revised downwards again, and poverty and food insecurity are rising. South Sudan holds one of the richest agricultural areas in Africa with fertile soils and abundant water supplies. Currently the region supports 10-20 million head of cattle. South Sudan is currently burdened by considerable debt, accrued largely in 2012, based on rapidly accumulating arrears, and increased military spending. South Sudan has received more than $4 billion in foreign aid since 2005, largely from the UK, the US, Norway, and the Netherlands. Following independence, South Sudan's central bank issued a new currency, the South Sudanese Pound, allowing a short grace period for turning in the old currency. Annual inflation peaked at 79.5% in May 2012 but declined rapidly thereafter, to an average of 1.7% in 2013. Following the December 2013 outbreak of violence, inflation is on the rise again. Long-term challenges include diversifying the formal economy, alleviating poverty, maintaining macroeconomic stability, improving tax collection and financial management and improving the business environment (2015 CIA WORLD FACTBOOK retrieved 08 August from:

(www.theodora.com/wfbcurrent/south_sudan/south_sudan_economy.html).

In the context of these failures, that may lead to complete disintegration of South Sudan nation-state. Hence, South Sudan would be required to embark on radical and meaningful reforms in the public sector. Radical change is needed so as to leave no stone unturned but doing it meaningfully in a way that the nation glues to the foundation of development and prosperity.

Institutional reforms as a recipe for reconstituting good governance

Cautious institutional change is what South Sudan desperately needs in the post Kiir-Machar conflict (2013). The nation had receded to the ancient age of tribalism, regionalism, and ethnicities. In the process, common national identity has faded away. Thus, it is necessary to embark on a regime of reform measures to curb the ongoing cry and adopt good governance. Some South Sudanese elites in the diaspora who are calling themselves, South Sudanese professionals in the diaspora, have highlighted key areas where reforms in South Sudan must begin. These include the rule of law, land, accountability, investment, army forces, taxation, asset recovery, public service and national constitution among others.

1. Applying the rule of law

Apparently, and concerning the rule of law, South Sudan has joined the rest of the failed world; where rules of law are not implemented and enforced in later and spirit. We have seen situations in South Sudan in recent days, were law supposedly enforcers committed unspeakable atrocities. In effect, the law breakers are protected and allowed to stay at large, none brought to justice. For example, the killers in Juba in what was called door to door Nuer- hunt to kill project, are still at large, the killers of the well-known writer, Isaiah Abraham have not been brought to justice, millions of dollars have been siphoned by people famous but, a zero number of these thieves have been brought to trial just to say a few. In my view, South Sudan Justice has collapsed in entirety. The South Sudanese professionals in the diaspora have proposed the below measures in anticipation to invent the culture of justice and fairness in the country. These include;

- **A national reconciliation process must be initiated headed by individuals with the moral authority to win the trust of the nation.**
- **A team of experts, preferably from outside the country should be invited to investigate the killings. Anyone found guilty and complicit in the murders, especially crimes against humanity, must face the full wrath of the law.**
- **The bedrock of our democracy must be the freedom of association enjoyed by the members of the public, freedom of press, the right to join a political party of one's choice without the fear of harassment by the dominant party or the security organs (Hakim et al. 2014, p.14)."**

I totally agreed with these measures, we cannot afford as a world's younger country, born lucky in the 21st century, surrounded by enormous opportunities to learn, adopt tested policies, but instead opted to remain a barbarous, failed and a police state. It is important to emphasize genuine national reconciliation. This could be done by making use of expert's knowledge to help in consolidating legal and justice parameters in the country.

2. Reducing land grabbing vice

Land is a natural asset that sustains human inhabitants; we cannot exist without land unless we become spirits that dwell in the airspace in which we are not. In South Sudan, land grabbing has occurred in two ways: firstly, few individuals grab both private and public lands for their use. These people encroach on the land that they think belong to nobody, Shirkat in Juba is a good example of a piece of land voluntarily taken over unpriced. Other grabbers bought the land cheaply from the private people who don't know the actual value of the property. The second layer of land grabbers are foreigners and companies, the people seized land through dubious means including bribing people in the authority to have quick access to a plenty of areas. A policy to eradicate this practice of land grabbing is overdue in South Sudan. Hakim et al. (2014, p.13), proposed the following as part of the earth's policy reform:

- **There must be a proper system put in place to ensure that the local people are adequately consulted before any piece of land is leased out to foreign companies or given to the government.**
- **Individuals or communities whose lands are elected should be compensated. Any compensation packages have to be done transparently.**
- **A specialized tribunal needs to be set up to deal expeditiously with issues of individual land grabbing including plots.**
- **Once there is cessation of hostilities, all current and old IDPs must leave the place they have taken refuge in, without any reservations. They should not be allowed to transform themselves into settlers or land occupiers, through the use of force. This is in the best interest of community relations.**
- **The government has a duty to ensure that the presence of IDPs in any area does not generate into forceful occupation of host communities' land (Hakim et al. (2014, p.13).**

3. Instituting proper taxation system

As stated by Online Business Dictionary, Taxation is defined as:

> "A mean by which governments finance their expenditure by imposing charges in citizen and corporate entities. It is argued that government use taxation to encourage or discourage certain economic decision. For example, reduction in taxable personal (household) income by the amount paid as interest on home mortgage loans result in greater construction activity, and generates more jobs for members of the public on job search networks."
> Sources: http://www.businessdictionary.com/definition/taxation.html#ixzz3iUL4ViqT)."

By this definition, one is acquainted with knowledge that a nation cannot render services without taxes. After all where else could money fall from to finance the daily expenditures of a government? It is rather an economic shock to have a nation without a proper taxation system. In the last few years after independence, South Sudan governments have depended on the following of oil as the main source of revenue making ninety-eight 90%). The fall of oil price connects with the fall of the economy in South Sudan because the two are intertwined. Thus, there is need to embark on proper and legal taxation system and market diversification in South Sudan. A nation cannot only depend on oil, as a fertile land country, but South Sudan is also potentially productive in agriculture, crop production, fish production, gold and animal husbandry, among others. The land of South Sudan is so rich that one could proudly say that even without oil, South Sudan could remain a prosperous nation more than a level of Kenya and Uganda, put together!

4. SPLM should not be a political party

Many people who have the focus in South Sudanese politics, these days have been bombarded with many coined Acronyms around SPLM. Truthfully, it has been a sense of confusion in digging to understand why do people defect from SPLM but later align themselves again with the SPLM regarding retaining the Acronym; examples in his context are SPLM-DC, SPLM_ OP, & SPLM-FD respectively. For clarity and layman consumption, SPLM stand for Sudan people liberation movement, SPLM-DC stands for Sudan People Liberation Movement for Democratic Change, whereas SPLM- OP stands for Sudan People Liberation Movement in Opposition, and lastly SPLM-FD stands for Sudan People Liberation Movement Former Detainees.

Under this heading (SPLM Must not be a political party), I shall explore historical origin of political parties, and unpack the significant reasons surrounding the importance of SPLM in the South Sudanese history of struggle and the context of political genesis of freedom, and as well as the current political dispensation of South Sudan as a new republic. I shall expose implications depicting why SPLM should not be a political party, but a common national identity that should be left with either national army or another state commonly shared ideology.

It is essential first to look at the origin of political parties in the world, their common ideologies so as to understand whether what we popularly call that South Sudan really fits in the context of world politics. The origin of political parties goes back to the 1600s. The ancient Greeks, who were pioneers in developing democracy, had no organized political parties in the modern sense. The Senate of the ancient Romans had two groups that represented people with different interests —

the Patricians and the Plebeians. The Patricians served noble families. The Plebeians represented the wealthy merchants and the middle class. Although these two groups often mingled, at times they voted for factions or parties, on particular issues that were relevant to the groups they represented. In Africa, the governing system used was chiefdoms, eldership and kingship along separate tribal groupings.

For many centuries after the fall of Rome (AD 476), the people of Europe had little voice in politics. Thus, there were no actual political parties — only factions that supported one noble family or another. Political parties developed as representative assemblies gained power. In England, this change began after what was called the Popish Plot of 1678. These narrowly based parties were later transformed to a greater or lesser extent, for in the 19th century in Europe and America there emerged parties depending on mass support. However, the 20th century saw the spread of political parties throughout the entire world. The political parties are guided by their ideologies; common in the global Western politics are conservatism and liberalism. For example, in the United States of America, the Democratic Party represents liberal ideals, while the Republican Party commonly represents conservative ideals.

Apparently in Africa, arms struggle was used as a major tool in the quest of independence in many countries in the continent. The arms struggle was predominantly the strategy used to unseat the colonial regimes. Contextually, after Sudanese (both Arabs & indigenous African) fought and achieved independently of Sudan in 1956. The South Sudanese was forced conditionally to wage second war for the independence of South Sudan. The independent which was later completed in 2011. Historically, the SPLM was born in the second phase of South Sudanese quest for independence it was thus a tool used to achieve South Sudan independence. Hence, SPLM was not meant to be a political party in scientific terms but an ideology meant to rally all South Sudanese around a common agenda which was then the self-determination of South Sudan with hope to culminate into total independence of South Sudan. The key word was liberation and movement. Naturally, it becomes inactive after independence. The question is liberation from what after independent? The following in my view has sharpened my intellectual impetus on opposing the existence of SPLM as a political party in South Sudan:

Firstly, SPLM has an outdated or already achieved mission that was a total liberation of the people and land of South Sudan. The independence was brought by a liberation movement carried by all South Sudanese people. This memorable and sacrificial work of all persons from all walks of life, from all creeds, faith, and gender cannot be narrowed to a single membership based entity.

Secondly, SPLM has become a source of conflicts, political bullying, and divisions with some cadres saying they are the 'real liberators' and questioning a patriotism of others who in a really sense contributed to the struggle just like them. It is clear from daily utterances from SPLM speakers that boosting on who did what during the struggle is the only slogan being repeated each day.

Thirdly, SPLM is using the gone war rhetoric instead of policies that enhance the social and economic development of a newly born country. It is not democratic in practical terms although democratic terms are used in pretense.

Fourthly, current SPLM is an old school based most of the powerful cadres in the current SPLM lack conventional knowledge of current political civilization. The world has moved from institutional power to people's power. Hence,

SPLM still holds to institutional power at the expense of people's power.

Fifthly, SPLM is still using what Professor Anyang Nyiogo of Kenya call a political militarism. They act as militants instead of using the power of political persuasion. Honorable members of parliament like to be referred to as 'Generals' instead of civilian politicians preferably.

Sixth, quitting SPLM is equated with the deleting history of struggle. Quitting SPLM is seen as the betrayal. It is this very reason that people leave SPLM but added in SPLM in their names (SPLM- DC, SPLM -OP, SPLM -FD) so that they are accepted or given credit for the struggle. These are a foundations set on falsehood rather than on ideologies. Having stated these, SPLM as a historical name that connotes the struggle of the people of South Sudan should be only instituted on a ground where all South Sudanese people should feel they belong to and embrace it proudly. Realistically, SPLM should only be aligned to a commonly shared identity. For example, the national army fit this very well or other institutions such veterans, etc. The rationale and benefit of taking off SPLM name in politics are to provide:

- Equal platform of all parties to compete on policies and strategies for social and economic development of South Sudan.
- Encouragements of parties that are now badly labelled as non-contributors to the war of liberation to active participate without intimidation.
- An opportunity for South Sudanese to see and practice politics.

As a SPLM file member, I believe that for the change to occur, SPLM must be repositioned, reconfigured, refocused to fit the current human political civilization or migrate it to commonly shared institutions. I also believe that a political party must be ideologically driven and that the membership of the party is crowded by people who identified with the party's ideology. Although ethnicity has shaped most of the African political parties, it is important for South Sudan, a country born lucky in the 21st century to embrace what I now call current human civilization.

5. SPLA should be made a conventional national army

The Sudan People Liberation Army (SPLA) was founded in 1983 as the military wing of the Movement (SPLM). The Founders including late Dr. John Garang had hoped that SPLA was meant to be a conventional armed rebellion, fighting to liberate the marginalized people of the Sudan in general and Southern Sudan in particular.

Indeed, the SPLA during the struggle for 22 remained committed to its founding principles and objectives (written in the Manifesto). It treated civilians with respect, followed rules of engagement in all battles. For example, there were more Prisoners of War (POWs) under the SPLA compared with non POW on the side of the enemy (National Islamic Front (NIF). However, after the independence of the Republic of South Sudan, the SPLA becomes diluted with elements from various untrained militias who were integrated into thousands in the SPLA proper. As a result, we now have the army that doesn't respect civilians and their properties. In his article entitled "Government: Stop creating more enemies, the veteran editor of South Sudan Mirror, Alfred Taban wrote this piece about SPLA:

A contingent of the Sudan People's Liberation Army (SPLA) burnt down houses and looted the properties of the people of Wonduruba. The army also returned to Katigiri and burnt it down. The people fled to safety to Lainya county, Dolo paya in Juba County and even to Jambu in Western Equatoria state. At least 10,000 people were displaced from their homes due to the army action. There is absolutely no justification for putting the people of Wonduruba and Katigiri to this kind of test. At this time when the peace agreement is being implemented, special attention should be directed to spoilers who want to scatter the peace deal. These soldiers who turned their guns on civilians are spoilers who should be held responsible for their deeds. The entire battalion that went to Wonduruba should be disarmed and investigated. Recruitment into the SPLA should now become a public issue with the communities each asked what kind of the people they want to join the army. Each community should name the persons they wish to join the army that should be deployed according to the wishes of the communities. A radical reorganization of the military is necessary. The current SPLA is the not the army of the people. It often works against the people. Reports of atrocities committed by the SPLA against civilians are numerous. Disciplinary action is rarely taken against the offenders. That means there are officers in the SPLA who are protecting these wrong doers. The SPLA should be turned from an army of robbers and crooks to a people's army, chosen by the people to serve the people (South Sudan Mirror, 2015).

Given the continuous atrocities committed by the supposed people's army. Many Citizens in South Sudan share the views expressed by Alfred Taban. In that, we cannot afford to have an army that sees civilians as threats and enemy. In the same way, we cannot continue to offer forty percent of our national budget to an army that turn guns to the funders (civilians). There is the need to train the army on conventional principles that define their duties and specifications. I am optimistic that SPLA can still gain its lost glory of being a people's army as it's used to be under late Dr. Garang de Mabior. This could be achieved after enormous work, and successful measures are put in place. These measures in my view may include, proper training, de-politicization and De-ethnicization of the national army, redeployment of the soldiers within the confines of the barracks that situated away from the cosmopolitan cities among other measures.

6. Establishment of Multicultural Commission

Given the multi-ethnicity of the South Sudanese people, there is great need to play a positive tune with diversity by forming multicultural department or call it commission that could handle promoting cultural diversity, through cultural events and festivals. South Sudan is a country of 64 tribes, groups of many cultural differences, beliefs and traditions. Hence, this diversity is good for the country regarding enriching the cultural fabric of South Sudan. In many countries such as Australia, there is a complete Ministry of Multicultural Affairs. This ministry is "responsible for advising the Government on all matters relating to multicultural and ethnic affairs in South Australia. The vision is to achieve an open, inclusive, cohesive and equitable multicultural society, where cultural, linguistic, religious and productive diversity is understood, valued and supported by all people (http://www.multicultural.sa.gov.au/)."

As South Sudan through recently signed agreement is expected to form Transitional Government of National Unity (TGNU), I believe that it is the right time to start the foundation of inclusive society by embracing common and shared identities. One of this is to incorporate a unified entity in the form of establishing a multicultural or ethnic commission, charged with responsibilities including advising the government on culturally, linguistically and traditionally concerns of the 64 tribes of South Sudan. The commission of multicultural affairs would annually celebrate cultural diversity and in so doing unite the people of South Sudan.

7. Establishing National Integrated Educational Curriculum

In many countries especially in Africa, education is a major factor in promoting national unity. It is believed that through education, students from different communities meet and forge together as one, people bonded by the power of interactive learning. In Kenya for example, Wandibba and Thuranira (2005) have stressed five factors that promote national unity in Kenya, these include; language, education, the constitution, economic integrations and social integrations (2005, 231).

In my view, these five factors have continued to cement the unity of Kenyan people and societies. As this has been good with Kenya, there is no profound reason education could not be a uniting factor for the South Sudanese. Although the geographical settlement of most South Sudanese appeared tribally regarding ethnic concentration in one area, for example in Lake State, only people of Dinka heritage inhabit the area. Similarly in Unity State, 99% of the people are from the Nuer tribe. In these States, the attendances in local schools were identified to be students from one ethnic group.

Thus, in this context, the national integrated educational curriculum could help by: Firstly, defined a percentage of students that could study in one school. This implied mix teachers and having students from other far away tribes coming to study in a particular school.

Secondly, the curriculum will teach significant of diverse cultures, traditions and beliefs held by each of the sixty-four tribes in the country.

Thirdly, the curriculum must expose tribalism as a negative factor that deteriorate national unity, prosperity and attribute it to all past failures as recipes of the practice of tribalism. In doing so, South Sudan in my view could be a cohesive country on earth.

8. Empowering traditional leadership structure

Traditional leadership in the African context is a significant discourse, especially regarding understanding the grass root style of governance in Africa. Although in the olden days, South Sudanese did not have traditional leadership structure. What used to exist was authority consolidated around the powerful groups or individuals.

Among those who held power in the place of recently instituted chieftainship were: Firstly, the mighty and rich men or clan in the community were respected. These people act as some sort of leadership in the community. In doing so, they could stop conflicts that are not in their interest or rescue any vulnerable people in society who might be harmed by others. Secondly, the magicians/Kujur or say the (Tiet/beny bith), who act as claimed influence of supernatural spirits. They were in some ways, revered as leaders with guidance. Thirdly, there were traditional kings in some tribes especially in Shilluk, Anyuak, Azande in the western and the Latuko tribe in the east who had at one point, kings but quickly disintegrated perhaps affected by divisions. These were three categories where elements of leadership existed.

However, the colonial era of the British Empire in Sudan /South Sudan in 1881 is credited to have founded chieftainship system of traditional leadership structure in Sudan/South Sudan. In the 1900s, the chieftainship helped then colonial governments in bridging people at the grass level with the government that was predominantly led by foreigners (British and Arabs).

Thus, my argument in this section is that the current government of South Sudan must embark on empowering traditional leadership structure. This empowerment could be done in the following ways: Firstly, the government should institute a House of Chiefs (HOC) in which the Head of State, seating president shall be the patron. The HOC shall among functions serve as a custodial of traditional customary laws of South Sudan. The HOC in my view can unify customs, traditions and beliefs of the sixty-four tribes of South Sudan. Secondly, transfer minimum constitutional powers to the office of the Chiefs. These include instituting chief police and giving full recognition of chief's court and matters resolved therein. Thirdly, maintain taxation collection at the rural settlement as work of the Chiefs. Fourthly, enhance support and respect for chief's work by awarding well deserving Chiefs in the annual Chief conferences held in the nation's capital, attended by all chiefs in the country and head of state or his or her representative.

9. Install federalism in the right time

Rush to federation cannot help South Sudan's grown chronic situation. The recent unexpected conflict in South Sudan has surprised many foreign nations and organizations especially those that have played crucial roles in both, nursing and creating the world newest country. The expectations of these nations were that South Sudanese given their experience in protracted wars were to be the last group on earth to take part in any conflict at a distance let alone the war within itself. They thought that South Sudanese people were only yelling for developments, education and the civilization of the entire nation. However, we proved them wrong that we were not a very people they had expected. Internally, South Sudanese were not at all surprised by this outrageous conflict. The signs and symptoms of such explosion were indeed a visible fact at the very eye of South Sudanese in the country and the diaspora. Figuratively, Dr. Majak Agoot (2014) referred to this as a boiling container of milk (known in Dinka as Ajop cui) when it has pressure inside it, and if such container's top is not taken off, there is the likelihood of bursting and exploding. This was what had occurred!! Nobody was able to open the container's top, unfortunately.

These signs and symptoms of then emerging conflicts were daily felt; from speeches among parliamentarians, incited cattle raiding such as in Warrap and Jonglei states, political incited ethnic and clans conflicts such as in Lakes State, Twic East County, land grabbing such as in Juba and in other major cities, disappearance or murder of journalists and outspoken civil society activists such as late Isaiah Abraham and Deng Athuai who narrowly escaped death, employment of civil servants based on their tribal alignment such as in many ministries in central government and states, and of course, the obnoxious uninterrupted corruption, etc. Interestingly, these unexpected levels of hatred that grew thick just within two years after independent precipitated what many analysts referred to as an ethnic war waged and spearheaded by politicians and army generals. South Sudanese from all political spectrums and communities appeared to have not fully understood the facts behind having an independent state and what it entails. Many people (outsiders) are asking whether South Sudanese were emotional, tribally and politically ready for an independence country or they each thought that South Sudan was to be their tribe owned state. Of course, each South Sudanese has the answers to these perhaps.

Optimistically, although we have lost thousands of our brothers and sisters, uncles, mothers, grandfathers, etc., in this baseless and needless conflict, we can still in effect forgive each other's prodigality and embrace oneness in the spirit of heavenly reconciliation. However, the process of reconciliation cannot be reached without a well-calculated framework; otherwise we can end having what could be referred to as Archbishop Deng-MaJak Agoot and George Athor, Peace Initiative. For those who have might not have come across this phrase. Dr. Majak and Archbishop Deng once offered in good faith with the blessing of President Kiir to reconcile Athor with the government; they reached out too late to General Athor to convince him to rejoin the government. Surprisingly, while they were on the edge of finishing negotiation, these peace makers plus late George were targeted for an Assassination by men of evil, and Athor has to rush them (Archbishop Deng and Dr. Majak's delegation) to their plane before bullets were to be rained on them. And indeed an attack was launched in General Athor's hide out while the plane was taking off.

In order not fall into the above scenario, the recent conflict must be solved amicably and truthfully within its right context. This brings me to my subject title that states that Rush to Federation Can Not Help South Sudan Grown Chronic Situation. In the media circles, especially from individuals and think tanks, suggestions are made on possible ways that the conflict in South Sudan could be best solved.

For example, Equatorians are calling for Federalism (Clement Wani, 2014), also in the recent media release of the SPLM-O led by Dr. Machar, Presidential Federal system is echoed (March 14,2014). Thus, in this paper and the following paragraphs I will briefly unpack how this notion of the so-called Federalism cannot help, molds this conflict. Hence, in this context, it is important to understand what a federal system is and how it is in most cases installed and applied.

Federalism is defined as a political concept in which a group of members is bound together by covenant (known in Latin as foedus, covenant) with a governing representative head. The term "federalism" is also used to describe a system of government in which sovereignty is constitutionally divided between a central governing authority and constituent political units (such as states or provinces). Federalism is a system based upon democratic rules and institutions in which the power to govern is shared between national and provincial/state governments, creating what is often called a federation.

Generally speaking, Federalism may encompass as few as two or three internal divisions, as is the case in Belgium or Bosnia and Herzegovina. In general, two extremes of federalism can be distinguished: at one extreme, a strong federal state is almost completely unitary, with few powers reserved for local governments; while, at the other extreme, the national government may be a federal state in the name only, being a confederation in actuality.

From this definition, one is convinced that South Sudan is not yet ready for the federation, and I have the following reasons to speculate. Firstly, South Sudanese does not have a collective bound of their own. They instead adhere to their tribal bonding. So there is the covenant within the tribal grouping then it would have one? National identity. Thus, if the federation is enforced, there is likely going to be a country with people that have no commonality at the national level.

Secondly, South Sudan at present is not democratically instituted; all we have been a bunch of cut and paste rhetoric statements of democracy. For example, in the last elections, there were rumors of rigging and subsequent rebellions as a result. The formulation of the transitional constitution was exclusive of the civil population; it thus became the document of the few elites, serving their entire political interests. In this situation, you cannot install federalism on thorny ground.

Thirdly, South Sudan has grown in recent few years, knowing that excessive use of power by the executive (especially President, governors, commissioners), experimented on daily cruel decrees of non- evaluative changes, dismissal of civil servants and subordinate executives with no publicly specified reasons. If this culture of baseless misuse of power is not first abolished nationally, then the federation will spread such obnoxious culture to all units of governments respectively. In Canada, Australia, USA and European, it is to be argued that as the years went on and these countries became bigger nations with absolute democratic rules, the citizens of these countries through their representative requested a better way to govern them that was when federalism was chosen and install after thorough public consultations.

South Sudan in my view is not yet ready for Federalism, and so frankly imported system of the federation cannot help South Sudan from its grown chronic situation. Alternatively, I believe that the recent conflict that has engulfed our entire community can and is solvable if the following are observed and implemented:

1. Immediate unreserved adherence to recently agreed Cessation of Hostilities (COH). This could be well achieved through the installation of aggressive monitoring Mechanism
2. a Full acknowledgment of responsibilities attached to the massacres on both sides of the conflicts. This includes surrendering evils perpetrators to relevant authorities for persecution. Although, the dead will not be resurrected, this gesture shall demonstrate a degree of honesty and accountability.

3. Formation of a Technocrats Interim Government (TIG) charged to expedite: reconciliation and national healing, permanent people's constitution, institutes good governance by restructuring institutions especially the national security and the entire organized forces. I agreed with Biar Ajak Deng Biar that both Kiir and Machar plus their fanatic' stooges must not take part in the interim government. However, they shall still be regarded as heroes who brought us freedom but failed their tasks on finishing- line.

4. Cooperate fully with world bodies requesting war crimes candidates and de-hostile neighboring countries who have for some reason meddled themselves in the conflict of the South Sudanese people.

5. Reduce the current extravagant and huge level governments in the Country, some departments in central government as well as counties and state programs must be amalgamated to give rise to development and efficient provision of Social services.

6. Establishment of Multicultural Ministry or department to cater for various cultural activities as a way to foster unity in diversity and parade yearly cultural days in the nation.

7. Install anti-corruption commission as directorate within the Ministry of Justice so that it has the tools and mandate to persecute vices in the country.

Finally, I believe that we are more than capable to resuscitate from the recent death and take our gloried place as a nation within the world of nations. We cannot afford to be a laughing stock in Africa and around the world. By all indicators, rush to Federation cannot help South Sudan from it grown chronic situation.

References

Agany, T. (2013, '). 'understanding the tribal, political and economic aspects of the current south Sudan civil war and their complications in achieving a peaceful, lasting solution. Sudantribune.

Alier, A. (1990.). *Southern Sudan: Too many agreements dishonored.* New York: : Ithaca Press.

Assefa, H. T. (1987). Mediation of Civil Wars, Approaches and Strategies-the Sudan Conflict. *Westview Press. Colorado:.*

Biar, M. Z. (2013,). *Z Tribalism in South Sudan,.* www.sudantribune/spip.php?article51002.

C, H. (2013). *History of christianity.* http://prezi.com/ows2ltegawpl/christianity/.

(n.d.). *Centre for alternative discourse manipur.* http://cad-manipur.org/in-focus/.

D Waddell, .. C. (2014). , *Organizational change: Development and transformation.* Cengage Learning Australia Pty Limited.

Deng, F. M. (2010). *Self-Determination and national unity, a challenge for Africa.* Asmara,: Saverance Publishing services.

Deng, JD 2014, why SPLM should be a political party in South Sudan. Sudan tribune http://www.sudantribune.com/spip.php?article52857

Demographics of South Sudan - Wikipedia, the free encyclopedia. (n.d.).Retrievedfrom http://en.wikipedia.org/wiki/Demographics_of_South_Sudan

Eprile, C. (1974.). *War and Peace in the Sudan, 1955 – 1972*. London: David and Charles.

(n.d.). *First Sudanese Civil war*. http://www.absoluteastronomy.com/topics/First_Sudanese_Civil_War

Forsberg, M. I. (1964). *Dry season : today's church crisis in the Sudan ; the development of the church in the Sudan, East Africa and the events leading to the expulsion of missionaries*. New York: Sudan Interior Mission.

Garang, J. (2005,). interview, no road in South Sudan since creation time".

H, B. (2013). *the Dangers of Tribalism in South Sudan*. https://www.chathamhouse.org/media/comment/view/196439.

Hirlinger, H. (2013). *What is 'tribalism' and why does is matter in South Sudan*. http://www.academia.edu/5517121/What_is_tribalism_and_why_does_is_matter_in_South_Sudan.

http://www.independentnetwork.org.uk/press/largest-number-independents-120-years. (2014). Largesr number of independent in 120 years standing.

http://www.southsudannation.com/proposed-. (2014). Proposed federal system for future South Sudan.

Index, F. S. (n.d.). http://library.fundforpeace.org/fsi14-overview.

Institute, w. B. (2014). *Fragile states*. https://wbi.worldbank.org/wbi/about/topics/fragile-states.

Johnson, D. H. (1979). "Book Review: The Secret War in the Sudan: 1955–1972 by Edgar O'Ballance". *African Affairs*, (310):132–7.

Kung, H. (n.d.). *Peace-Tripod*. http://lumpykarma.tripod.com/images/peace.html.

Lagu, J. (2006). *Sudan: Odyssey through a State (From Ruin to Hope*. Taylor and Francis Ltd.

little education is sickness. (n.d.).

Mahathir Mohamad, (. P. (2001). Malaysian Prime Minister) address during the World Evangelical Fellowship.

(n.d.). *management guide*. www.managementstudyguide.com/training-of-employees.htm).

Mayardit, K. (K 201). Presidential Speech at 1st Independence of South Sudan. *Presidential Speech at 1st Independence of South Sudan*.

Muzna, S. (2015). The role of media in today's world. http://www.hamariweb.com/articles/article.aspx?id=10166.

O'Ballance, E. (1977). *The Secret War in the Sudan: 1955–1972*. Hamden,: Connecticut: Archon Book.

(n.d.). *Prayer and l war*. http://kuyah.blogspot.com/2009/01/prayer-war.html.

(n.d.). *Religiously based civil unrest and warfare*. http://www.religioustolerance.org/curr_war.htm.

(n.d.). *Sudan conflict* . http://www.insightonconflict.org/conflicts/sudan/conflict-profile/.

(n.d.). *Sudan history*. http://www.anasudani.net/english-5.html.

(n.d.). *Sudanese civil war*. http://mapyourinfo.com/wiki/en.wikipedia.org/the%3DFirst%3DSudanese%3DCivil%3.

T, D. (2015). Conflict in the church.

Turabi, H. (2013). *Interview on the wake of 2013 south Sudanese conflict.*

Ugaz, J. (2014,). *Corruption is threatening economic growth for all.* Transparency International.

Waanglicana. (2013). https://waanglicana.wordpress.com/2013/05/14/a-war-we-cannot-afford-to-loose-tribalism-in-kenya.

(n.d.). *Why do you believe in god?* http://www.shroomery.org/forums/showflat.php/Number/10629734.

(n.d.). *Youth against Tribalism in African.* http://yatia.cfsites.org/custom.php?pageid=37000.

(O'Ballance, 1. S. (1999.). *War and Conflict in Southern Sudan, 1955–1972. PhD Dissertation,,.* Santa Barbara.: University of California.

(OCHA), O. f. (2013). http://www.unocha.org/.

Omondi C.F 2015 Fight to win against tribalism; http://www.the-star.co.ke/news/article-121039/we-must-fight-win-war-against-tribalism

Poggo, S. S. 1999. *War and Conflict in Southern Sudan,* 1955–1972. PhD Dissertation, University of California, Santa Barbara.

Scott, K 2015, Accountability in South Sudan cannot wait for peace, Amnesty International South Sudan https://www.amnesty.org/en/latest/news/2015/07/op-ed-accountability-in-South-Sudan-cannot-wait-for-peace/

United Nations Economic and Social Commission, Good governance http://www.unescap.org/sites/default/files/good-governance.pdf

www.ingramcontent.com/pod-product-compliance
Lightning Source LLC
Chambersburg PA
CBHW030445300426
44112CB00009B/1175